Beatle Family Trees

by

Colin Gardner

All rights reserved. No part of this publication may be reproduced, distributed, or transmitted in any form or by any means, including photocopying, recording, or other electronic or mechanical methods, without the prior written permission of the copyright owner, except in the case of brief quotations embodied in critical reviews and certain other non-commercial uses permitted by copyright law. For permission requests, write to the publisher, addressed "Attention: Permissions Coordinator," at the Amazon Kindle website contact address.

Copyright © 2021 by Colin A Gardner

All rights reserved. This book or any portion thereof may not be reproduced or used in any manner whatsoever without the express written permission of the publisher except for the use of brief quotations in a book review.

Although the author and publisher have made every effort to ensure that the information is correct at press/publication time, the author and publish do not assume and herby disclaim any liability to any party for any loss, damage or disruption caused by errors or omissions whether such errors or omissions result from negligence, accident or any other cause.

Beatle Family Trees

If I May Be A Little Foreward..

The Beatles will live on through history, there's no doubting that. Together, they achieved so much and people will always find something to write about them as they remain constantly fascinating and enigmatic. Thankfully, so much of the Beatles story has been recorded on film, on record, in books and more, as a band or themselves as individuals. Their lives have been documented every which way possible it seems. My last book, Beatleplaces tried to source and detail the formative part of their early lives. Where they were brought up, went to school, where they met, who they knew, where they played and more and hopefully thus explain what made them the individuals they became who in turn, became the Beatles. Their family is a large part of this and so now I've researched the Beatles family trees. In one interview Paul gave he said his family were "just very ordinary people" and that "I've met lots of people but never anyone as interesting, or as fascinating, or as wise as my Liverpool family.". I hope the evidence of this book will let you find that out too.

I was not the first and I will not be the last person to attempt this but I have researched the McCartney, Lennon, Harrison and Starkey family trees going back beyond their parents, which tends to be the limit on most Beatle biographies. I have used the best resources available to me and my local knowledge to give you (as it gave me) an insight in to these "ordinary people". Hopefully my details stand up to scrutiny and I hope in the process I've cleared up a few myths and provided you with a few surprises too along the way. Enjoy. C.G

Chapter 1 - John Lennon's Family Tree (Paternal side)

1800- onwards

Great, Great, Great, Grandfather Lennon

Patrick Lennon- Farmer- born approx 1800 - County Down, Ireland
Elizabeth Lennon – Wife - County Down, Ireland

Married: Unknown

Sibling- (known)
James Lennon - born 1829 -County Down, Ireland

There's no evidence of the actual location in County Down where Patrick Lennon came from. Irish census and related records were very basic in this era and not much can be determined from them. The Lennon surname and its' variations were common in the county. Patrick and his wife are only known because they are mentioned by their first name only on James's marriage banns when he married in Liverpool in 1849. There are no details of other brothers or sisters to James either. In 1845 Ireland suffered its famous Potato Famine causing masses of Irish families to emigrate to England, Canada and the U.S.A and one such person was James Lennon who left Ireland for a better life and moved to Liverpool around that time, possibly 1847/8. There's no evidence so far that his father Patrick, left Ireland too. Being a farmer he had good cause to leave though.

The research I've attempted on Patrick "Pat" Lennon has been varied based upon the little details we have and without more is virtually impossible to validate but by all means have a go yourself. These are the hits I've made.

1847- Patrick Lennon recorded on Griffiths Valuation property tax list in Drummiller, Aghaderg, Down (agriculture and property)
1858- Patrick Lennon- Drumgath, Dromore, Down - died
1805-1883 Patrick Lennon died- Newry
1812-1892 Elizabeth Lennon died- Newry.

1849- onwards

Great, Great Grandfather Lennon-

James Lennon- 1829 – 1898 -County Down, Ireland
Jane (McConville) 1831 – 1869 - Dromore, Aghaderg, Newry, Down, Ireland

Married: 29/4/1849 at St.Anthony's Chapel, Scotland Road, Liverpool
Living at Vauxhall Road/Saltney Street- Liverpool

Jane McConville's family seemed to have left Ireland for Liverpool together as her father James, mother Bridget and brothers, John and Richard were registered as living in 54 Saltney Street too.

1851- Census

James and Jane were living along with two other families in 51 Saltney Street, Princes Place, Liverpool with their daughter Elizabeth born in 1850. James was a merchant warehousemen. This location was mostly made up of poor immigrant housing just feet from the Clarence Dock and graving docks and offered cheap, available labour force for the ship owners. The next road to Saltney Street was Dublin Street where the Beatles posed for publicity pictures in 1962 and it hadn't changed significantly up to then.

1861 Census

The Lennon family had now moved a few hundred yards away to 3 Paget Street, close to Nelson and Bramley Moore Dock. They shared the little house with the Fagen family. James was now a warehouseman cooper (making barrels). It was a tough, hard, deprived neighbourhood but James and Jane managed to raise a family there. By 1861 the family included Elizabeth (1850), James (1853), John (known as "Jack") (1855), William George (1858) and Richard Francis (1861). Jane's mother Bridget McConville (now a widow) joined them. Elizabeth, James and John were scholars and knew how to read and write which improved their chances significantly.

John "Jack" Lennon was John Lennon's grandfather.

1871 Census

The Lennon family had moved once again (and probably times in between) to live at 31 Eldon Place, Liverpool in the Vauxhall district where there are many records of McCartney's and Lennon's relatives living in this area throughout the 19th and 20th century. Their position had improved significantly by 1871. They now had a servant girl Martha Carr from County Tyrone, Ireland and had three boarders (all Irish).

Jane had two more children by 1869. Joseph born 1865 and Edward born 1867. Sadly, the Lennon family suffered two tragedies between 1861 and 1871 also. Daughter Elizabeth died in May 1866 aged just 15 and was buried in Ford R.C Cemetery, Bootle (D475). In January 1869 Jane Lennon died aged just 36. She too was buried at Ford R.C Cemetery, Bootle (RF450). Mother in law Bridget was still living with them. James Lennon was now 42 and a warehouseman. His son James was a warehouse keeper. John "Jack" had used his education to become a railway clerk. Richard was a scholar and elder brother William was a scholar and a boarder at St Edwards College, St Domingo Road. This was a Catholic institute and a junior seminary and much later he joined the priesthood.

1881 Census

Something had changed by 1881. James Lennon (now a widower) was lodging at 2 Pownall Square, Liverpool living above a provision shop run by Mr. Moses Jones and family. Son John "Jack" had since married in 1879 and left the family. (More on him in full later). Son William George was also no longer with the family, training to become a priest and had progressed from St Edwards College, Liverpool then Urshaw College Durham and Spain and he possibly over to Ireland (More on him later too). 15 year old son Joseph was now a saddlers shop boy (located at 18 St Anne's Street) and lodging in an all-male lodging house at 121 St Anne's Street, Islington containing over 120 males. This now left James with sons Richard and Edward. James was still a warehouse porter, as was son Richard.

1891 Census
More changes for the Lennon clan. James now lived at 373 Walton Breck Road, Anfield in his own home. He declared his occupation as "manager for a car company" (tram cars) which was distinctly different to his other jobs and possibly allowed him to get the house. Indeed the house still exists today and is still a motor garage. James son Edward and his wife Ann were living with him as well as two young nephews Richard and Edward Lennon.

1898
Now living with his son John "Jack" at 12 Caradoc Road, Seaforth, North Liverpool, James Lennon died aged 68. He was buried at Ford R.C Cemetery along with his wife (and later Mother in law Bridget and son James) in plot RF450.

The Lennon Ancestors (Great Uncles)

Before I summarise the John Lennon's grandfather, John "Jack" Lennon, I'll deal with his brothers firstly.

Joseph Lennon 1865- 1928
1881 census he was 15 and working as a saddler's shop boy in St Anne's Street Vauxhall
May 1884 he married Agnes Walker aged 20. He was 19 but declared himself 21 years old. He was shown now as a mechanic by trade living at Oriel Street, Vauxhall
1885 Son James Joseph Lennon born and in 1887 son George Lennon was born.
1901 census the family were living at 13 Aden Street, West Derby, Liverpool. Joseph was now a marine fireman, Agnes was a charwoman and their sons were errand boys in a bottling store.
1911 census shows they had moved to 6 Tulloch Street, Kensington, Liverpool. Joseph was a dock labourer now. James was still at home and a carter. George had become an able seaman/labourer/leading signalman with the Royal Navy. His service record shows he had active service from 1903 through WW1 into 1923. The service record even reports the tattoos he bore, a pair of crossed hands and heart and a woman's hand holding a rose on his right forearm.
1928- Joseph Lennon died aged 64 years old. He was a painter by trade in that time. He is buried at Anfield Cemetery S15 No: 1152

Richard Lennon 1861- 1932
1881 census shows Richard was living as a lodger with his widowed father and brother Edward above a provision shop at 2 Pownall Square in Liverpool city centre. He worked as a warehouse porter.
1889 July he was living at 373 Walton Breck Road, Liverpool where his father was now the manager of a tram car business. He married Ellen Burns from Rupert Hill, Everton in 1889. The ceremony was performed at St.Francis Xavier church (SFX). His brother William George Lennon officiated the ceremony as an ordained priest, though he wasn't based at SFX.
1891 census Richard was an ironmonger's shopman and living at 2 Letterstone Street, Everton.
1899 Richard and Ellen had a daughter Honorah (Norah)
1901 census and Richard was living at 52 Robarts Road, Walton. He was now working as a book-keeper for a marine engineers.

The 1911 census shows that Richard had done well in his change of job. Now secretary to an engineering company, he had moved "over the water" to the Wirral living at 31 Grosvenor Street, Liscard. It was probably a work-related move but now he and his family had a domestic/servant working there. (This semi-detached house was only 100 feet from the Beatles venue Grosvenor Ballroom, Grosvenor Street, Liscard, Wallasey.)

1918 to 1932 Richard relocated back to Liverpool, living at 77 Priory Road, Anfield. In 1925 his daughter Norah married Francis S Thomson, a dentist who worked in the same road. (Norah later left Merseyside and lived in Bolton until her death in 1996.)
In 1928 Mary Ellen Lennon died and in 1932 Richard Lennon died. He was buried in Anfield Cemetery in a private grave Section 4 No: 1066, possibly with his wife.

Edward Lennon 1867-1944
1881 census shows that 14 year old Edward was lodging with his father James and brother, Richard above a provision shop at 2 Pownall Square, Liverpool. Like his brother, he worked as warehouse porter.
1889 March. Edward married Ann Jane Rigby at SFX church but brother William George was not officiating (he may have been overseas)
1891 he was living with his wife and two children Richard and Edward at 373 Walton Breck Road with his father who managed a tram car company. Edward was a car driver. This was a horse-driven car/tram.

1901 census- Edward and family had moved to live at 14 Job Street, West Derby. Edward was a coachman/groom. His eldest son Richard (14) was now an office boy. The siblings now comprised, Richard, Edward (12), Joseph (9) and daughters Mary (7), Ann (3), Elizabeth (2), Florence (2m).
The 1911 census reveals the family had increased even more and they had moved. They were living at 26 Dee Street, West Derby. Edward had two further children, daughter Francis (9) and son James (2). Edward was still working with horses and coaches as a harness cleaner.
1914 the family were living at 18 Palatine Street in West Derby. As WW1 began son Joseph, an engineer at this point enrolled to join the Infantry (Kings Liverpool Regiment) but was discharged soon after (5 days) as unsuitable "not likely to be become an effective soldier".

The 1939 register reports that Edward was still living at 18 Palatine Street with his wife and daughter Florence. Edward was now a retired corporation watchman. His daughter Florence though married, was living with her parents and worked as a theatre barmaid.
1944- January Edward died at Sefton General, 126 Smithdown Road, Allerton (where Julian Lennon was born). He was buried at Yew Tree Cemetery (Plot 2C 286), West Derby. His wife Ann joined him there when she died in 1951.

Daughter Florence appears to have married twice Her first husband, Thomas F Fitzgerald was a merchant seaman on M.V Apapa whom sadly drowned. Florence lived at 24 Redrock Street, Liverpool 6 until she was widowed. Her name is shown as Florence Nilson on the 1939 register and had indeed re-married. She lived at 26 Toft Street Liverpool until her death 1980.

James Lennon 1853-1888

1871 census James (2) was living at home at 31 Eldon Place, Vauxhall Liverpool and he was a warehousekeeper.

In 1875 he was now living at 19 Haigh Street, Everton and in February 1875 he married Ellen Ford from Abram Street, Everton at SFX church, like his brothers Edward and Richard.

The 1881 census shows he had moved to 21 Paley Street, Anfield and had three children, Jane (1874) Elizabeth (1876) and James (1878). His grandmother Bridget McConville was also living with them. His occupation was a provision merchant shipping clerk.

In August 1888 aged 35 James (2) died. He was buried at Ford RC Cemetery Plot G165. His cemetery record showed he was last living in 35 Upper Pitt Street which signifies he had moved to a poorer residential area for reasons unknown.

Following the whereabouts of his widowed wife Ellen, the 1891 census shows that she moved to 11 Bachelor Lane, Horsforth, Yorkshire with her daughters Jane, Elizabeth son James and their great grandmother Bridget. There's no known Yorkshire connection but Ellen, Jane and Elizabeth had gainful employment as silk spreaders. There was a silk mill industry in that part of Yorkshire but the big move there seems more more typical of the journeymen artisans of the time.

When Bridget McConville died she was returned to Liverpool and buried at Ford Cemetery with her daughter Jane. Ellen died in Wharfdale Yorkshire in 1923. Ellen's children all married and remained in Yorkshire.

William George Lennon 1858- 1921

William was the first to leave the Lennon family. He appeared on the 1871 census as a boarder and scholar at St Edwards' College, St Domingo Road. Everton. This was a Catholic institute and junior seminary with an international reputation of training young men to become catholic priests and Christian missionaries. William's college included other scholars training for the priesthood, some from as far as Peru, Brazil and Portugal. The college had its own Bishop in residence, priests, maids and even a butler.

There's no census report for 1881 but the likelihood is William was abroad around this time but not before some further training for the priesthood based at Urshaw College Durham and possibly a stint in Maynooth, Ireland. The Roman Catholic Diocesan Archives indeed show he went as far as Spain during this time.
William appeared back on official records in 1888 when the Reverend William G Lennon was given a clerical appointment in Ainsdale, North Liverpool.

In 1889 he was officiating priest at SFX church when he married his brother Richard to Mary Ellen Burns but his actual church was St Joseph's Church, Serpentine South, Blundellsands North Liverpool, near Southport in Lancashire (Same road as Brian Epstein's assistant Alistair Taylor) . He was living Harlech Road, Great Crosby during his stint there which was 1890 to 1905. He seemed to have also had a stint working from St Nicholas Church.

The 1891 and 1901 census shows William was now an ordained Roman Catholic priest and shared the accommodation with a housekeeper,Lucy Kavanagh. Lucy was born in 1858 in Wicklow, Ireland (previously living at 38 High Street, Wicklow, Ireland). The 1901 census included her sister Rose as a "visitor" but she was there quite regularly. Rose came to England and initially worked as a housemaid for a family in Clapham, London. She later became a ships' cook/stewardess on transatlantic voyages travelling Liverpool to Boston or New York City on a regular routes run by the "Devonian", "Cestrian" and "Canadian" right up until 1913. There appears to be some evidence that Rose was frequently discharged from ships and may have spent some time in a London infirmary/workhouse and this may have signified some issues which came to light later.

Reverend William Lennon also seemed to have had some issues of his own in the early 1900's. Commentators and family have suggested that he possibly had a nervous breakdown and mental illness leading to a drinking problem. There was always speculation that he may have also had a relationship with his housekeeper, Lucy. It was said there was a fall from grace but he was on record as Reverend William G Lennon –Priest on a record held in London St Pancras Board of Guardians Religious Creed Register of August 1905, which shows that William was admitted for care there. He was case 75 and held on ward 5, admitted from the Edwards Hotel. He was referred there by Reverend Wilfred Foley, priest at St Aloysius, 49 Clarendon Square, London. Wilfred may very well have been an old college friend/associate whom he turned to. Beatle fans will know of St Pancras Hospital as it appears in the Beatles famous "Mad Day Out" photo session on 28 July 1968 when they were photographed in the flower bed of St Pancras Hospital Gardens, little knowing of John's great-uncle William's sad past there.

William returned to Liverpool and possibly on advice from his brother Richard who was living in Liscard, Wirral at the time, he moved there too, living in a modest terraced house at 52 Albermarle Road, Liscard. His devoted housekeeper Lucy joined him there. There was a Roman Catholic church Our Lady of the Sea/St Joseph's on nearby Wheatland Lane, Wallasey which he may have worked from.

The 1911 census has two points of interest. Lucy Kavanagh was living at 52 Albermarle Road, Liscard, declared as the "Head". She also had taken in boarders but at this time there was no sign of Reverend William George Lennon. Lucy's sister Rose had quoted this address as her home on several ship manifests when she worked as a ship's cook, so she may have lived here too for periods. I found William Lennon on the 1911 census taken at the same time elsewhere. He was shown as a lodger in Brownlow Cottage, East Cowes, Isle of Wight on that date. This may have been a place he went for health/convalescence reasons but I can't prove this.

There are no more available U.K census after 1911 yet and the only known record is the death of William George on 26 August 1921 aged 63. He died of broncho-pneumonia at 52 Albermarle Road, Liscard and his faithful housekeeper Lucy was present at his death. He was buried in the family plot at Ford R.C. Cemetery, Bootle Plot RF450.

In February 1931 Rose Kavanagh died. She died at Hundred Acre Mental Hospital Barnstead, Middlesex. Her body was brought up to Ford Cemetery by her sister Lucy. She was placed in her mothers' (Mary) grave in Ford Cemetery N111. In August 1934 Lucy Kavanagh died. She had lived at 52 Albermarle Road from 1905 until 1934. She was also buried in Ford Cemetery, Bootle P375 but the grave is no longer there and may have also been added to her mothers' grave plot.

Grandfather Lennon

John "Jack" Lennon 1855-1921

John "Jack" Lennon is John Lennon's paternal grandfather. His own life was eventful and tragic on numerous occasions but the stories from his surviving sons give the impression of a "happy go lucky" man who enjoyed company and entertaining, especially in pubs around Liverpool. The stories that have emerged from that may have been enhanced, embellished with re-telling and even imagined to a large degree based upon the merest of details. I'll show you the research I made into these "facts" and you can judge the rest. He was without doubt though a true Liverpool character and a lot of his traits are evident in grandson John Lennon's life too.

First thing first, John "Jack" Lennon was not born in Ireland as a lot of books report. (even the Pauline Lennon biography of Fred Lennon says this). He was born in Liverpool 12 January 1855 and baptised at St.Nicholas's, Copperas Hill, Liverpool. This church was just 200m from where his son Alfred would marry Julia Stanley in Bolton Road in 1938 and 210m from Mount Pleasant Registry Office where John Lennon married Cynthia Lennon in 1962. Some census records (i.e. 1881 reported John "Jack" as from Ireland but the likelihood is that the landlord may have assumed this when completing the census.

The 1871 census shows the last occasion John "Jack" was with his family. Living at 31 Eldon Place, Vauxhall, Liverpool, 16 year old John "Jack" was already working as a railway clerk.

In May 1879 John "Jack" married Annie Skalley (born 1853) and in the same year they had a daughter Margaret Jane which suggests Annie was pregnant before the marriage. They lived with Annie's parents at 24 Upper Milk Street, Vauxhall and in 1880 they had a son William George and another daughter in 1881 Mary Ann. All three children had very sadly died by 1881. The 1881 census reports John "Jack" was living at 24 Upper Milk Street still and he was now employed as a labourer.

In September 1882 Annie Skalley died. She died of phthsis, which is a kind of pulmonary tuberculosis. The slum living conditions, sanitation and cramped housing in industrial areas like Liverpool and Birkenhead from as early as 1800 was a terrible plight on young and old and mortality rates were high. Ringo's own great grandfather died in his 20's of T.B in Birkenhead. Annie Skalley was buried in a public grave at Anfield Cemetery Plot S3 No: 1070.

On 19 August 1888 John "Jack" Lennon re-married. He married Margaret Cowley (1866) at Our Lady Of Immaculate Conception church, Everton. Before I give further details on this we have to account for the 6 years between Annie Skalley's death and John "Jack" remarriage in 1888. There's not much detail to be found as census records fell either side of this period. This "wilderness period" allows us to speculate what he did in the interim.

Many Beatle researchers and historians have mentioned that John "Jack" Lennon was a member of a travelling minstrel singing group called "Andrew Robertson's American-European Original Coloured Operatic Kentucky Minstrels" and that he toured the United Kingdom, Ireland and even the U.S.A. It was further suggested when went to the U.S.A and performed there and that he even married there and had a child, whom he brought back to England. The facts I've gathered are these. There certainly was a theatrical troupe by that name and it was a very popular act in its time when "Blackface" acts were a big box office draw. "Blackface" involved white men blacking their face to perform negro songs and other lively tunes of the day.

Following the death of his first wife Annie, he could have been free to pursue a musical career. No electoral roll evidence has yet come to light showing an address for him between 1882-1888. His family were living in Pownall Square in 1881 and just before his marriage in 1888, John "Jack" was definitely living with his brother Richard at 3 Stanfield Road, Anfield. Though the Kentucky Minstrel troupe existed, I don't think it was active during 1882-1888. The adverts and publicity I found indicated that they were touring U.K and Ireland predominantly around 1892 onwards at which time, John "Jack" was married and working in Liverpool. The Kentucky Minstrels were a performing troupe of at least 30 artistes who were "blackface" entertainers whom sang burlesque, carols and even operatic tunes in addition to dancing and farce. It's reported that the troupe also included some actual black artistes from America, which is unusual in itself. Minstrel singers often accompanied themselves on banjos or the like and being operatic minstrels I'm sure an orchestra helped out here.

The publicity I've tracked down from the 1890's reported them playing several shows a week in places like Barry and Newport, South Wales, Limerick and Dublin in Ireland and Scotland. The troupe appeared to have performed in Liverpool in October 1893 as a charity benefit show and no publicity gives mention of any performer's names. The impresario Andrew Robertson of the named troupe can't be found either. The troupe publicity did however claim to be "Direct from America" and critic's articles were very complimentary of the show in places like Ardrossan and Preston. "Xceedingly Xhilerating" was one. "The Eiffel Tower of Minstrely" was another.

So the Kentucky Minstrel troupe existed but it doesn't tie in with John "Jack's" wilderness years. Furthermore, there are no emigration records found of John Lennon leaving or returning from the U.S.A. with a wife or child, so the touring American stories are unfounded. The whole minstrel singer myth may have emerged from a single photograph of John "Jack" Lennon that can be found online. In it, he's stood in a top hat and tails next to a white man holding a banjo in minstrel type "blackface" makeup regalia. John "Jack" looks about 25 years old and it looks posed against a theatrical backdrop. There were no Kentucky Minstrel photographs found, only typed publicity and press reviews. And I wouldn't say therefore that this one picture constitutes a whole singing career. The wilderness years 1882-1888 remain intact.

On 19 August 1888 John "Jack" Lennon married for the second time. He married Margaret Cowley who lived at 41 Hamilton Road, Everton. The marriage certificate suggests John "Jack" was living with his brother at the time in nearby 3 Stanfield Road, Everton. Margaret was pregnant 5 months at the time of the wedding. On 1 December 1888 Mary Elizabeth Lennon was born at 28 Minera Street, Everton.

The 1891 census found the John Lennon family of John, Margaret and Mary had moved out of Liverpool. Work, or lack of it most likely the cause. They re-located to 63 Allen Street, Warrington, Lancashire as boarders of Holloway family. In 1888 John "Jack" was noted as a millers' book-keeper. Now, in 1891 he was a railway clerk. The annual census for 1891 was held on 5 April. On 8 May 1891 Margaret gave birth to twins. John and Annie at Walton Workhouse,(which was an infirmary as well as a place for paupers and the destitute). This signifies that John and family had moved back to Liverpool. They remained in Liverpool into 1892 as John and Margaret had another child Margaret on 19 August 1892 at Walton Workhouse again. Childbirth was dangerous and unsanitary in the 19th century and this proved to be with Margaret who sadly died in childbirth. Margaret was buried in a Roman Catholic public grave, Everton section 12/189. This left John "Jack" Lennon with three children to care for, one newborn and twins under 2 years old as well as his first daughter Mary Elizabeth. Even more tragedy befell John "Jack" Lennon when his daughter Ann died in December 1892, then younger daughter Margaret died in September 1893 and the remaining twin John died, June 1894. Annie was buried in a pauper's grave at Everton Workhouse S9 294. The burial details for Margaret and John are unknown but I would assume these too were pauper's graves in Walton, West Derby or nearby.

In 1894 John "Jack" Lennon began living with Mary Maguire. Mary was born in 1871 in Liverpool and hailed from 42 Whitford Street, West Derby. Like John "Jack", she had Irish parents who emigrated to England about the same time as James Lennon. The next available official record of them both was the 1901 census but a lot had happened between 1894 and 1901. They had not married but Mary had given birth to 6 children who all died young. This included three children all named John. It was not uncommon to re-use the name if a child died. These children were John (died 1895), John (2) (died 1895), Walter (died 1898), John Arthur (3) (died 1898), Catherine (died 1899- 24 days old) and Beatrice (died 1901). All the children were buried at Ford Cemetery but in separate plots, possibly public graves with other young children.

The Lennon's had 15 children together in total and only 7 survived to adulthood. During 1898 John "Jack" was resident in North Liverpool living at 12 Caradoc Road, Seaforth possibly during the latter days of his father's life and may have cared for him. The 1901 census also showed that John's first daughter Mary Elizabeth was still with him. The old and new family were now living at 3 Lockhart Street, Toxteth Park. John "Jack" was now a shipping clerk. John "Jack" and Mary (known as Polly) were not married but various baptism records from 1894 onwards show "Mary Lennon" as the mother.

Between 1901 and 1911 census the Lennon family moved again to 24 Denton Street, Toxteth around 1904/5 and by 1908 were living in 27 Copperfield Street (Dickensland), Toxteth. John "Jack" was a freight clerk. He and Mary had more children together, William (died 1902), Leonard (died 1902) George (1905), Herbert (1908), Sydney (1909), Harold (1910), Alfred (1912), Edith (1915) and Charles (1918). George died in 1911.

Alfred was John Lennon's father.

The 1911 census reported one change in the household. John "Jacks" first daughter Mary Elizabeth, (born to his 2nd wife), Margaret had left. I located Mary Elizabeth Lennon living at 11 Belvidere Road, Princes Park, Liverpool 8. This was the address of Liverpool High School, a girl's public day school trust and boarding house. Mary was one of the many staff there and at 22 years old she was a housemaid/waitress there. Beatle historians have drawn a line over Mary Elizabeth Lennon after 1901 and had presumed she married or emigrated. There's no genealogical evidence of a local marriage or even further afield for many years after 1901 and on the emigration theory there were a LOT of Mary and Mary Elizabeth Lennon's emigrating and they were invariably from Ireland. There were two emigration records which give her full name but little else holds up. One record shows a British citizen left Liverpool on the "Scandanavian" (Allan Line) for St.John, New Brunswick, Canada February 1916. This Mary Elizabeth Lennon was aged 24 year old (born 1892) and a domestic. This is a person 4 years older than our Mary Elizabeth Lennon regretably and the notation on the ship manifest says "off", so she may never have gone in fact. I traced one other emigration record found however dated 21 August 1930 showing a British person called Mary Elizabeth Lennon who appeared on a Naturalisation Register in San Francisco U.S.A. If she was this person she would have been 42 years old at the time of application, not a likely age to emigrate.

I did however find local Electoral Records around 1938 to 1940 showing a single Mary Elizabeth Lennon living at 46/48 Mount Vernon Convent run by Irish nuns called The Sisters of Mercy with an all-female attendance of approximately 35 ladies. It's not clear if this Mary was part of the staff or an actual nun but considering that Uncle William George was a fully ordained priest it has strong potential that she may have joined the convent.

The latest record for a Mary Elizabeth Lennon I found was circa 1963 and 1964 when the name appears in the electoral register at the Convent of Mercy, Broughton Hall, Yew Tree Lane, West Derby. This was a convent/preparatory school run by the aforementioned Sisters of Mercy. Later on the convent withdrew as a school and a dedicated R.C school was built on the grounds. So it seems to suggest this may be our Mary Elizabeth Lennon who began her working life in girl's schools and **may** have remained in schools via convents as a nun. Her religious followings aren't known but the family observed Roman Catholicism and her Uncle Reverend William may have been an influence. Her death can't be confirmed thereafter and she may have even been buried on site and the convent order do not provide personal information quite rightly. Research on this is ongoing.

In January 1915 John "Jack" formally married Mary "Polly" Maguire at a registry office in West Derby. This was very belated as marriages go and after two previous church weddings it seems unusual to opt for a registry wedding but with so little money and a lot of children, possibly it was easiest. Oddly, the given address on the marriage certificate is 27 Elmore Street, Everton. This turns out to be the home of Mary "Polly" Maguire's married sister Catherine. John "Jack" also gave his occupation as "dock labourer" on this occasion. The address and occupation may have been a ruse and a lot of Beatle related certificates have little inconsistencies like this.

Now married for the third time, John "Jack" Lennon and family were established at 27 Copperfield Street, Toxteth from 1909 as records go. He was working as a freight clerk for Booth Shipping based at Harvey Building, 33 James Street, Liverpool just by Liverpool Pierhead. Booth Steamship Co. Ltd owned a small fleet of ships that imported rubber and leather from Brazil and even kangaroo meat from Australia. Harvey Buildings was next door to the corner sited building Albion House at 30 James Street, with iconic striped red masonry owned by The White Star Line who owned "Titanic". John "Jack" was working next door at the time of the announced Titanic disaster and the White Star Line staff were afraid to go outside their building following the news and read out the names of the deceased from the balcony of the office to the crowds below and John "Jack" would have been aware of this and very probably saw it.

The last remaining record of John "Jack" Lennon was his death 3 August 1921. He died at home in 27 Copperfield Street with his wife present. He left 7 surviving children, one of which was Alfred Lennon father of John Winston Lennon some years later. John "Jack" Lennon was buried in Allerton Cemetery in an unmarked public R.C grave Section 4 No:206, which he shares with five adults and three children of no relation. The interment record for the grave show he was buried 6 August 1921 at a cost of £1 and 13 shillings. The funeral directors were William McLean & Sons Ltd, 206 Windsor Street, Toxteth Liverpool 8 which was just 25 yards from his home in Toxteth.

John "Jack" Lennon's family

Mary "Polly" Lennon remained at 57 Copperfield Street for the rest of her life. She died February 1949 of myocardial failure and a bronchial congestion, a typical illness in the polluted industrial air of Toxteth and Dingle. She was cremated at Liverpool Crematorium.

George Lennon (son) born 1905 - died 1956
Herbert Lennon (son) born 1908 – died 1968
Sydney Lennon* (son) born 1909 – died 2003
Alfred Lennon (son) born 192- died 1976 (John Winston Lennon's father)
Edith Lennon (daughter) born 1915- died 1980
Charles Lennon (son) born 1918 – died 2002

Sydney Lennon emigrated with his wife in the middle 1960's. He died in 2003. He is buried at Mount Pleasant Cemetery, London, Middlesex County, Ontario, Canada. Section CM (Columbriam) Wall. Alfred Lennon has a well-known documented past. He was a sickly boy with rickets. He was lucky enough to become a day boarder at Bluecoat School, Wavertree with his sister Edith. He left there to finally become a steward on the merchant ships regularly sailing from Liverpool and gained a reputation as an entertainer and "happy go lucky" chap much like his father. He met 15 year old Julia Stanley in Sefton Park one summer day and they began to see each other much to her family's objection. They dated nearly 11 years. They finally married in 1938 in a registry office in Bolton Street, Liverpool and whilst "Freddie" was at sea in October 1940 Julia Lennon had his son, John Winston Lennon on 9th October 1940. The rest you probably know.

Chapter 2 - John Lennon's Family Tree- (Maternal Side)

The consequence of so much research and investigation into family trees should hopefully be something new and hopefully interesting. I concentrated on the more well-known Irish lineage of Paul McCartney and John Lennon mostly but inevitably other family roots were involved and worth a mention and provided more than a few surprises with it. None more so than John Lennon's maternal family tree.

The Millward and Stanley Family Trees

The Stanley Family Tree

John Lennon's mother Julia was the fifth daughter of George Ernest Stanley and Annie Jane Millward.

The Stanley family hailed from Lambeth, London who then moved to Birmingham, Warwickshire then onto Liverpool in the 19th century.

The Millward family came from Chester, Cheshire and Flintshire & Denbighshire of North Wales and they too moved to Liverpool in the late 1800's.

William Henry Stanley (2) was born in 1814 and baptised at St.Mary's, Lambeth, London. He was the son of stonemason William Stanley (1) and Isabella Stanley.

William Henry Stanley (2) became a carpenter and lived in James Street, Lambeth , London. He married Elizabeth Miller in September 1833 at St.Anne's Church, Soho, London. They had three children.

Edward Herbert Stanley. Born 1838 in Lambeth, London
Eliza Stanley. Born 1845 in Birmingham, Warwickshire (possibly later married in Warwickshire)
William Henry Stanley (3). Born 1846 in Birmingham, Warwickshire

This move to Birmingham sometime in the 1840's suggests that William Henry Stanley (2) was a journeyman carpenter coinciding with the development of Birmingham's canal and rail systems during its' Victorian era industrial boom and yet he stopped his trade and took up clerical work as a solicitor's clerk instead, which is a big difference. It proves William Henry Stanley (2) was able to read and write and so had an education as a well as a skill. More surprises were in store however.

The 1851 census shows that family had moved to the St.Michaels' district of Coventry. William Henry (2) was now a General Solicitors Clerk.
The 1861 census reports that the Stanley family had now settled in Chilvers Coton, Nuneaton, Warwickshire. Wife Elizabeth had since died and he was now a solicitor's clerk with his son William Henry (3) and daughter Elizabeth left in the household.

The first of the Stamley family to reach Liverpool was Edward. Son Edward had since moved up to Liverpool. He was now a clerk in a steam ship company and he lived in Everton. He married Catherine Bentley Cooper, (another Londoner) in Birmingham in 1856 and they moved up to Liverpool after that. They raised a son William Herbert. It seems that they split up and she went to live with her mother (also relocated in Liverpool). Kate/Catherine never re-married and died in Bootle aged 94.

Edward remarried on September 1866 in Liverpool. He wed Mary Ann Gildea from Ireland. The 1871 census shows they had a son also called Edward.

The 1866 marriage certificate is dated September 3 1866 and the ceremony was conducted at St Simon's Church, Liverpool now showed that Edward Herbert Stanley was stated as a "Mariner" though on several items he was a Quay Clerk or Freight Clerk. Weirder still is that he names his father on the certificate as William Henry Stanley (2) (b 1814) but quotes his father's profession as "**Actor**". I've seen numerous certificates were details like this are bogus, exaggerated somewhat or plain misheard but more on this entry will emerge as you'll read.

Edward's brother William Henry (3) may have come to Liverpool at the same time but he was living in Liverpool by 1868. William Henry (3) married Eliza Jane Gildea, the sister of Mary Gildea who had married his brother Edward two years earlier. The marriage certificate declares his father William Henry Stanley (2) was a "Clerk" this time around.

The 1871 census indicated that William Henry (3) and Eliza had now settled in Liverpool. He was a solicitor's clerk and they had a child also called William Henry (4). At the same time, William Henry Stanley (2) was reportedly still living in Chilvers Coton and working as a "clerk" himself.

The 1881 census had more to report. William Henry Stanley (3) was living in 12 Cadmus Street, Everton. Eliza had declared she came from Omagh, County Tyrone, Ireland. (Later census revealed this was actually Drumragh, Omagh, County Tyrone.) The Stanley family had enlarged and she had 4 sons. William Henry (4) born 1869, Arthur Charles born 1872, **George Ernest** born 1874 and Frederick James born 1879. The census also commented that they had William Henry Stanley (2) now aged 67 as a boarder on that date and is declared as a widow and "solicitor's clerk- out of employment". It suggests he was in the care of his son and daughter-in-law and hoping for work in the area.

The third son, George Ernest later married Annie Millward who raised several children including Julia Stanley, John Lennon's mother. **George Ernest Stanley is therefore John Lennon's maternal grandfather**.

In October 1881 William and Eliza had another son, Albert John Stanley. The baptism record reports his father William Henry Stanley (3) was a warehouseman.

November 1882 saw the sad loss of youngest son Frederick John Stanley aged 3 years. He was buried in a group grave at St. Mary's Cemetery.

The 1891 census revealed some more changes. William Henry Stanley (3) was not there. Eliza was head of the family though stated she was still married. They had moved from Everton to the inner city district of Abercromby, living in shared accommodation at 143 Upper Frederick Street. Only George Ernest and Albert were still living at home. George Ernest was now an errand boy.

In 1892 Eliza Jane Stanley married an Anton Abrahamson in Liverpool. BMD records confirm the names but no more has been found on this gentleman (possibly a Swedish/Norwegian sailor). This implies that William Henry Stanley and Eliza had divorced prior to 1892 as he was not dead (later evidence I found of him working in Durham- see later). The 1891 census shows she was "married" but Anton was not there. The 1901 census reports a widow called Eliza Abrahamson and had 2 children, a 16 year old Charlotte Stanley daughter and a son Albert living at 15 Cornwallis Street, Liverpool . So Anton may have died sometime between 1892 and 1901 very sadly

In 1894, William Henry Stanley (2) passed away in Chilvers Coton, Nuneaton, aged 80. He obviously returned to his first family home and retired there.

The 1901 census summary found shows Eliza Jane living at 56 Chester Street, Toxteth as a lodger. and all her sons had left her.

William Henry Stanley- the first musician

Looking for missing William Henry Stanley (3) I found him on a 1901 census quoted as a "visitor" at a boarding lodge 2 City Road, Prince of Wales Beer & Lodging House, Peterborough, Northants. He declared his occupation a "musician" working on his "own account" and gave his birthplace as Birmingham and his age matches (54). He also reports he is married. Just to make things curiouser the next name on the census in the same lodgings is an Ellen Stanley, aged 56, occupation cook, also married but not reported as a wife. She hailed from Norwich, Norfolk. This name and her details have been investigated but found no trace of her before or after.

Wondering about the possibility of William Henry Stanley (3) pursuing a musician's career, I found a 1902 County Directory for Durham, South Shields entry which quotes a William Henry Stanley-musician living at 44 Derby Street, Durham. Therefore, if William Henry Stanley (3) was a musician, the Peterborough record indicates he may have been touring the area and the Durham record establishes some kind of permanent musicians job in that area. There is a 1914 directory record of a William Henry Stanley living at 106 Newbottle Street, Houghton Le Spring, Durham but trade stated as shopkeeper now and no subsequent death record of that name in the area. To date, no more can be traced about William Henry Stanley the professional musician.

In October 1906 son Albert John Stanley married Sarah Arnold. He was a tram car conductor by employment. He quoted his father William Henry Stanley's (3) occupation as a "shipwright" (ship carpenter) on that occasion. You can see how the records fluctuate so.

In November 1906 son George Ernest Stanley married Annie Millward at St. Peter's Church, Liverpool. They were both resident in Cornwallis Street, Liverpool (in the Chinatown section of Liverpool). In stark contrast to his brothers' marriage certificate George quoted his own occupation as "mariner" and his father's occupation as "**musician**" which helps confirm the findings of 1901 and 1902. It also typically indicates whether the father is deceased and on this document, he wasn't suggesting he was still around in 1906.

There's precious little to be found for the remaining brothers Arthur Charles Stanley and William Henry Stanley (3) after this time. I believe William remained in Liverpool and may have been a fireman circa 1901. As for Arthur C Stanley, I only located that name regarding an admission record to an asylum October 1908 but nothing can be confirmed.

There's one last entry found for Eliza Jane Stanley. She appears on the 1911 census. Living at 56 Chester Street but no longer a boarder, she is head of the house, aged 60 using her previous surname Stanley once again (it's not clear if there was any stigma with the Jewish surname) and reportedly a widow. She even stated she was married 38 years up to then. She also states she has two relatives in residence, Charlotte Phayre aged 25 (confectioner) and allegedly a daughter, plus her (granddaughter) Irene Elizabeth aged 9 months. This indicates that a daughter was born in 1886- full name Charlotte Gildea Stanley but she doesn't appear on the family 1891 census. This also shows that William Henry Stanley (3) was still a husband/father up that time.

It's been found that Charlotte was living with Eliza Jane Stanley's brother, (a poulterer in Hunter Street). Interestingly, the Gildea family had another niece in residence, Mary Ann Blackburn who was a domestic/servant there. She was born in Bengal, East Indies. Just to make things complete, the baptism record for Charlotte has been found and on it her father William Henry Stanley occupation is "mariner". Charlotte married in 1910 and her marriage certificate shows that she lived in Lime Street and on this occasion her father was shown as a "commercial traveller" so the documents are very random about William Henry Stanley (3) the musician.

Eliza Jane (Gildea) Stanley died in 1916 and is likely buried at Toxteth Park Cemetery. As for William Henry (2) no death record could be traced.

The Millward Family Tree

The maternal lineage to John Lennon continues and this time we look at his Welsh roots.

The Stanley family made some significant moves from Lambeth London to Birmingham and then settled in Liverpool. Likewise, the Millward family came from North Wales, moved to Chester on the English/Welsh border and finally settled in Liverpool. The surname is recorded in two variations on available archives Millward or Milward.

George Ernest Stanley married Annie Jane Millward in 1906.
They had 7 children.

Charlotte Alice Born 1899 – Died 1900
George Ernest (2) -Born 1903 - Died 1903
Mary "Mimi" Elizabeth - Born 1906
Elizabeth Jane- Born 1908
Annie Georgina - Born 1911
Julia   Born 1914
Harriet - Born 1916
(Charlotte, George Ernest (2) and Mary "Mimi" were illegitimate/ born out of wedlock.)

It seems best to look at the Millward family tree going back firstly from as early as records allow.

1800'S – Mary Elizabeth (nee Morris) Millward

April 1851 Mary Elizabeth Morris is born in Berth-Y-Glyd, Llysfaen, Colwyn Bay. It's situated along the North Wales coast and is about roughly halfway between Liverpool and Bangor. Her parents were William and Ann Morris (nee Davies). William was a farmer in Llysfaen.

It's said that young teenage Mary Elizabeth Morris had to leave the farm due to having a child out of wedlock with a neighbour's son. The neighbour's son never acknowledged being the father. The next found record was a 1871 census report.

The 1871 census found 20 year old Mary Elizabeth living as a housekeeper in Bridge Street, Llangollen, North Wales with her reported grandfather Samuel Williams, a widowed man aged 80 and formerly a carpenter. Odd that the grandfather is a "Williams" but neither her father or mother were of that surname. Mary also stated she came from Llangollen, North Wales. She co-resided there with her sister Jane Anne Morris, who was a dressmaker. This may indeed have been a refuge for her if there had been a birth out of wedlock.

Between 1871 and 1872 she met John Millward. The encounter came about because it's said that John was an apprentice solicitor's clerk to the Williams family (led by Sir John Hay Williams who were substantial land owners in North Wales) and in his early twenties he suffered a gun injury during a hunting expedition when he lost his left arm as a result. It's further said he took convalescence in the seaside town of Rhyl but this may possibly have been temporary and he went to Llangollen which is further inland and nearer Chester and Liverpool. Llangollen is and has been a picturesque Victorian tourist spot and Bridge Street, Llangollen in particular has many hotels and pubs and lodgings.

In 1872 the couple of Mary Morris and John Millward had their first child, Annie Jane. She was born in Chester, Cheshire in lodgings at what later became the Beer and Billet Inn, 94 Lower Bridge Street, Chester (right by the River Dee) which is still there. The move to Chester, Cheshire England from Wales just next door may again been because of being pregnant and unwed and they may have posed as a married couple which confounds as they could have just married but this may have been because of something in John's past rather than Mary's. More on this when we follow John Millward's history.

Sometime during 1874/1875 John and Mary and Annie moved to Liverpool.

By 1881 census the "Millward" family were established in Liverpool. Clearly because the work was there to be had and they could begin anew. They were living in tenements at 17 Kent Square, Liverpool. John was a clerk in a law stationers' office. They now had three children, Annie Jane (1872- Chester) now 8, Mary Elizabeth (1875-Liverpool) now 6 and Harriet (1877-Liverpool) now 4.

There are some stories about Mary Millward which may outline her personality that came to the fore with Annie Jane's daughters (Mimi, Julia and all) in later years. It's been said that Mary Millward was a powerful matriarch and she refused to speak English, calling it "The Devil's Tongue" and preferred Welsh. There was a Welsh Presbyterian/Calvinistic Church in nearby Princes Road, Toxteth (still there) and she made sure her family attended there regularly. Her Welsh upbringing and strong religious ties seem all the more reason why any alleged illegitimacy be frowned upon by farm folk in Wales and reinforces the question of their need to move to Liverpool.

The 1891 census shows another change in circumstances. Mary Millward was now living alone in lodgings at 18 Sussex Street, Toxteth, near Dickensland. She was "married", aged 38 and a dressmaker, which would fit as her sister was working as one in Wales.

Daughter Mary Elizabeth (2) was still living with her father as his own census reveals. She married in 1892 so left him. Daughters Harriet and Annie are nowhere to be found in 1891 but may have been together I suspect.

It's believed that just after the 1891 census John Millward died of a stroke and was found days later. By 1901 Mary Elizabeth Millward was now living as a "widow" with daughter Harriet who returned to the official records. They were living at 20 Kent Square, Toxteth. Harriet was a fancy box maker.

Harriet married in 1903 and a few years later emigrated to New Zealand (more later).

The 1911 census is the last available census record of Mary MIllward. She was living in 206 Beckwith Street, Birkenhead now, "over the water" living as a charwoman. The community of Beckwith Street was exactly like the Toxteth and Dingle area, docklands and housing and lodgings.

In 1932 Mary had moved back to Liverpool and was resident at 71A Berkeley Street. She died in 1932 and was buried in Allerton Cemetery Public Grave S32 1151.

1800's - John Millward

An interesting man with a lot untold. John Millward was born 1838 in Wales. His parents were Thomas and Jane Millward. They lived at Roe Street, Parish of Talar, St.Asaph, Denbighshire.

Thomas (b.1806) was a head gardener for Sir John Hey Williams, the High Sheriff of Flintshire. This was a prestigious post and gave the family some status. Wife Jane (b.1810) was from Nantglyn, Denbighshire.

The first evidence of John Millward (Milward) was on the 1841 Welsh census. Living in Talar. He was 7 years old and had 3 other siblings Thomas, Elizabeth, Mary. More family followed after this.

NOTE: Thomas Morris died 1882 and Jane Morris died 1887. They are both buried at Old Cemetery, Mount Rd, St.Asaph H4A South.

The 1851 Welsh census advises that the family location remained the same and the family were all still living at home. Thomas was now a carrier. Brother Edward was a shoemaker, his sisters were still at school and John was now an attorney's writing clerk. This apprenticeship was to the wealthy Williams family his father worked for, managing their legal matters. John's birthplace is quoted as Bontnewydd. Previous Beatle historians have commented that John was born on the grounds of Dolben Hall (probably a tithe cottage for his gardener father) in Bontnewydd, St Asaph.

Aged approximately 25, John Millward appears to have left home and was now **married**. He appears on the 1861 census living at Shaw Villa, Rectory Street, Wordsley, Kingswinsford in the West Midlands. He describes his occupation as "gentleman" (a person with no occupation but who derives income from "interest of money" i.e. savings/investments). He also proves his background by confirming he was born in St.Asaph, Denbighshire. He is married to Jane Millward (maiden name not found) who came from Montgomeryshire, Wales. They also had a servant named as Elizabeth Turner (married) as a housekeeper but was admittedly the sister of Jane.

The Millward name originated in the West Midlands/Shropshire so there may have been a family tie still active for John Millward to associate with.

I found no marriage records from 1850 to 1861 for John and Jane nor could find out what made John Millward move to this location. This first marriage has never been noted before. There is no evidence of a death of Jane Millward or if he even divorced. How he acquired "interest of money" or title "gentleman" is hinted at in the news article I found regarding his shooting accident. I researched this incident and found various newspaper articles in the local Welsh press.

Flintshire Observer 10 February 1871 & Denbighshire Advertiser 4 February 1871
"Gun Shot Accident"
A young man, belonging to this place (St.Asaph) named John Millward now living at Rhyl on money left him, lost his arm on Thursday week (2 February 1871) through an accident with a fowling piece. It appears he went in company with some persons in a rook shooting and when between Pengwern Lodge and St Asaph having the lock of the gun between his legs, he was somehow showing his talents when the piece went off, the discharge lodging in his left arm, which was amputated at Rhyl that evening by Drs. Jones & Roberts and for a time the unfortunate young man's life was in danger.

The title of "gentleman" appears in the other articles I found for John Millward when St Asaph Petty Sessions were reported in other local newspapers around this time.

Flintshire Observer 13 January 1871 published the following article.

St. Asaph- at a special sessions held on Friday last before Capt. Thomas and Whitehall Dod Esq., John Millward described as a "gentleman" was charged by Mr. Francis Wynne, Clerk to the Guardians with disobeying an order of the Justices to pay 5 shillings weekly towards the support of his father and mother. For not complying with the order which had been made, he was fined £2 and 14 shillings costs and a warrant of distress to issue at once unless the money was paid.

Flintshire Observer 10 November 1871 -published the following article

St Asaph Petty Sessions- Before Capt. Thomas and Whitehall Dod Esq.

Charles Grimsly, collector of the guardians of the St. Asaph Union, summoned John Millward of Rhyl to show cause why he had not complied with an order made upon him to pay 5 shillings weekly towards the maintenance of his parents, who reside in St. Asaph. The defendant pleaded that the collector had not applied to him personally but merely through letter and that he would not pay because he had not the means. A warrant of distress was granted.

The matter continued into 1872 it seems as the following press article appeared.

North Wales Chronicle- 13 July 1872

Proceedings were ordered to be taken against Mr. Millward, Rhyl for refusing to maintain his parents.

I am gauging from the clippings seen that this is our John Millward from the locations mentioned. It also seems his parents were in need of support and therefore poor, whereas John Millward had funds but wasn't planning to give them away, even after court warrants. His move to Liverpool seems to be on the basis that this money ran out or there were marital complications. This money may have come from his connections with the Williams estate (who lived in Pengwern Lodge), evident with companions mentioned at the gun shot incident or his first marriage or a will from a relative, possibly in the West Midlands. These all seem to have changed once he'd left for Liverpool.

I found a death register record for a Jane Millward 1864 in the Leek and Staffordshire area which may be reason for the return to Wales shown on the 1871 census.

The 1871 Welsh census (April 2 1871) reports that John Millward is now a widow and aged 35 living at 30 Water Street, Rhuddlan, Rhyl, North Wales. His occupation is now "interest of money" i.e. a gentleman and not working for a living. He confirms his birthplace is St.Asaph, Denbighshire and he occupies the property with his housekeeper from his Wordsley address, Elizabeth Turner (66) named as a sister in law validating it's the same man. Elizabeth confirms her birthplace as Montgomeryshire and also states Llanwrog, which is a coastal village in Gwynned, Caernarfon, possibly an old marital address. The address also has a local, young resident aged 16, Elizabeth Jones occupation cook. She hails from Rhyl. This may be the convalescence house mentioned about by Beatle historians but we know future wife Mary Morris was some distance away in Llangollen at the time. Possibly she left Llangollen and ventured to the busier bustling coastal town of Rhyl after 1871.

The story of John Millward continues to confound as I found that in October/November 1871 a John Millward married an Elizabeth Jones in Denbighshire. This John Millward person was much older, born in 1815 and a widower but also a "gentleman". His own father was a grocer and I think this may be a link and credence to the rich uncle mentioned by the Stanley family when they began to acquire properties in Liverpool some years later.

The marriage of John Millward to Mary Elizabeth Morris was sometime around 1871/4. The great Beatles historian Mark Lewisohn has quoted in "Tune Out", that John Millward described his occupation as "gentleman" which connects with the 1861 and 1871 census found so far and validates this is the same man.

The other John Millwards'

Before the story continues its worth clarifying the other people called John Millward who have been assumed to be the husband of Mary Morris and should be dismissed.

John Millward, Llanwit Major, South Wales. This person's father was a publican. The North Wales and South Wales locations were too big a difference.

John Dumbry Millward- hailed from South Wales, Glamorgan. He later joined the Welsh Infantry and fought in WW1. No census seen from 1881 onwards in Liverpool when John was definitely with Mary did he quote his Dumbry name or even an initial.
The other myth is that John Millward had such status and that he was awarded "Freeman of the City of Chester" (when he lived there briefly). The Chester.Gov website will show you all the appointed freeman on their historical register and there is no Millward/Milward unfortunately. This may have been a family myth as Julia Lennon (John's half-sister) quotes John Millward as John Dumbry Millward and the freeman title has been stated in her memoirs and unfortunately don't stand up to scrutiny.

1871 onwards-

John Millward and Mary Morris met and married between 1871 and 1874. However and wherever they met they moved to Chester in Cheshire, England. This period fell between census reports so nothing can be established in terms of what they did or where they lived although one residence has been recorded. They lived/lodged at The Earl of Shrewsbury's (Charles Henry John Chetwynd-Talbot- 18th Earl up to 1877) town house (now the Bear & Bill Inn), Lower Bridge Street, Chester. The Inn is still there facing a row of pretty Georgian houses on cobbled roads heading down to the River Dee.
It was the 18th Earl who had a castle built in Alton, Staffordshire in the mid 19th century and it coincides with John Millward being located near to it around 1861.

In 1873 John and Mary Millward had their first child together. Annie Jane Millward was born in Chester at the Earl's townhouse in Lower Bridge Street. Their next child was born in Liverpool in 1875 so it's unknown what brought about this change from what seems a comfortable location in a prosperous area and most notably with some status, as a gentleman and connections with the peerage to hardship and struggle in Liverpool. But the Millward family moved nonetheless and they next popped up on the 1881 census in quite different surroundings.

The 1881 census shows that the Millward family were living in shared accommodation at 17 Kent Square, Toxteth Park, Liverpool. It was a poor area of Liverpool. Kent Square had Kent Hall Mission in the middle of it.

The people who lived there were mariners, dock labourers, shipwrights, sailmakers and clerks. John Millward declared his occupation as a clerk in law stationers, which befits him in his earliest job in Wales as an apprentice attorney's writing clerk. They now had three children, all girls. Annie Jane, now 8. Mary Elizabeth (2) now 6, and Harriet now 4. Mary and Harriet had been born in Liverpool placing their arrival time in Liverpool around 1875.

Things had not boded well for the Millward's compared to previous times. The 1891 census showed even more revelations.

The 1891 census reported that John Millward was now lodging at 71 Highfield Street, St.Paul's district near Vauxhall as a boarder with his daughter Mary Elizabeth (2) with him. His wife and other children were not on the record. He was now a clerk in a merchants and oddly declared himself as a widower from "Ryle" (Rhyl). Mary Millward was still quite alive as it goes. Mary Millward was now living alone in lodgings at 18 Sussex Street, Toxteth near Dickensland. She stated she was married and a dressmaker. She was living away from the rest of her family. Annie Jane and Harriet could not be found in this period.

The 1901 census shows that Annie Jane Millward was living alone from the family at 62 Frederick Street, working as a seamstress.

It's supposed that John Millward later died of a stroke (possibly 1893) alone in his lodgings and wasn't found for days. I didn't find a death record for anyone in that period. His enigma remains.

The children of John & Mary Elizabeth Millward

Mary Elizabeth Millward born 1875. Married in 1892 to John Connor (Carter). They both lived in Hunter Street, Islington, Liverpool. They later moved out to 49 Norfolk Street, Bolton and later on, Laburnum Road, Denton, Lancashire. Possibly due a death or divorce, Mary returned to Liverpool and lived at 8 Cadmus Street, Liverpool until her death in 1964.

Harriet Millward born 1877. She married Patrick Mathews, an Irishman (from Knockdinnon, Dunleer) in 1903. He was also a Roman Catholic and as a result mother Mary Millward disowned her and her whole family of 3 children, Eliza, Richard and Patrick Jr. For a short while Harriet and Patrick lived in 18 Bismarck Street, Everton but on 15 October 1909 they emigrated to New Zealand on the Cunard ship "Athenic". They settled in Mauriceville, Masterton, Wellington and prospered, raising 9 children. Harriet kept up pen pal correspondence with sister Annie Jane and later it was John's Aunt Mimi who kept up correspondence with the cousin she never met, son Patrick. They finally met when The Beatles toured New Zealand in 1964. John's Aunt Mimi arrived by plane and stayed with her relatives in Levin, Horowhenua. She stayed with her other cousin Annie Parker (nee Mathews) her husband and their 4 children for a few weeks, obviously meeting up with all her distant relations. She also gave the children tickets to see the Beatles play their afternoon gig at the town hall in Wellington on 23rd June 1964.

Annie Jane Millward born 1873 (BMD Chester 8A 367). Annie married George Ernest Stanley 19 November 1906 in Liverpool. By then they had already had three children out of wedlock. She had 7 children but two died young. Charlotte Alice and George Ernest (2). Five girls remained.

Mary Elizabeth "Mimi" Stanley- born April 1906- Liverpool
Elizabeth Jane "Mater" Stanley- born 1908- Liverpool
Annie Georgina "Nanny" Stanley- born 1911- Liverpool
Julia "Judy" Stanley – born 1914 - Liverpool
Harriet Stanley - born 1916 – Liverpool

Julia Stanley was John Lennon's mother

George Ernest Stanley- Banjo mystery

Many, many Beatle books and websites make mention of Lennon's banjo. This is the El Dorado of Beatle musical memorabilia. If it exists still, it would be worth a lot to anyone who owned it. The background to the famous artefact is that John's mum Julia played a banjo herself, taught by her dad **George** who bought the banjo. She in turn, encouraged a teenage skiffle-mad John to learn it too. When John played with the Quarry Men using an acoustic guitar, he used banjo chords simply because he didn't know any different. In 1958, Julia Lennon sadly died and after that, there is no mention of the whereabouts of the banjo which must have held massive sentimental value to John. There is no photographic evidence of what the banjo looked like but comments from other Quarry Men who saw it, have stated that the banjo had a mother of pearl backing. The other fact is that the elusive banjo was bought sometime in the 1930's. Researching the possible origins of the banjo, you need to look towards John's grandfather, **George Ernest Stanley**. Up until the mid-1930's, George was a merchant seaman and records show he was working on several ships including the **"Cuban"** as a 23 year old in 1896-97, reporting into New Orleans for trade. More significantly in 1932, records show George was a 56 year old working on the merchant ship, **"Patrician"** which sailed from the U.K to Georgetown, Demerara in British Guyana and took provisions again to **New Orleans** and back. Given the huge musical heritage of New Orleans, early jazz, Cajun and boogie-woogie, it's quite likely George brought a mother of pearl backed banjo back from "The Big Easy" in 1932. It's just my theory however. Now that the Stanley family tree has revealed musical roots there could even be the suspicion that his grandfather and father may have acquired the instrument.

Annie Jane (Millward) Stanley died 26 April 1941 and was buried in Allerton Cemetery 28 April 1941 in the General plot Section 4 grave no: 376.

George Ernest Stanley died 2 March 1949 and was buried at Allerton Cemetery 7 March 1949 in the **CH 39 Section No: 777** which for no known reason, is nowhere near his wife's plot.

The children of George Ernest & Annie Jane Stanley

Mary Elizabeth (nee Stanley) Smith 1906 – 1991

Known as "Mimi" to her family. Married George Toogood Smith in 1939. She had no children but became guardian of her nephew, John Lennon in 1946 when her sister couldn't manage. She was a dominant force to be reckoned with as can be told in many Beatle biographies. Her husband George died in 1955 and she never re-married. She brought up John and when he married she refused to attend. When John found world fame she remained at the family home for several years until grateful John bought her a bungalow in Poole, Dorset and where she stayed until she died in 1991.

Elizabeth Jane (nee Stanley) Parkes, then Sutherland 1908 – 1976

Known as "Mater" to her family. Elizabeth "Mater" Parkes was the sister of John's real mother Julia and his Aunt Mimi. First married Captain Charles M Parkes. Charles Parkes was a marine surveyor who ran a marine survey business Hicks & Parkes- 4th floor, 42 Castle Street, Liverpool 1. In the early 1930's, he married Elizabeth Jane Stanley, elder sister to Julia and younger sister to Mary (Aunt Mimi). Elizabeth was also known as Mater or Betty. She was John's aunty. Charles and Mater moved to "Ardmore" 486, New Chester Road in the mid-1930's and the house became a regular rendezvous for the entire Stanley family. Mater had a son, Stanley and he lost his father at an early age. During World War 2, his mother met Bertie Sutherland, a dentist in Preston, Lancashire. Bertie & Mater married in 1949 and moved to nearby Fleetwood, a coastal town in Lancashire. They first lived at 33 Galloway Road, Fleetwood where John came to visit as a young boy. Later, the Sutherlands moved onto nearby 90 The Esplanade, Fleetwood and John came to visit there too but in due course, the Sutherlands upped sticks and moved all the way to Edinburgh. John continued to visit until he was 16 and later visited them with his future wife Cynthia. John always loved seeing his family and Scotland. Aunty Elizabeth died in 1976.

Annie Georgina "Nanny" (nee Stanley) Cadwallader 1911- 1997

Anne was a civil servant for many years. She married late, marrying Sidney Cadwallader in 1946 and they lived across the River Mersey in Rock Ferry in the house previously owned by her sister Elizabeth. Anne was known in the family as "Nanny". As a young boy, John visited Anne with his Mother often and played with his half-sisters there as several photographs have shown; including the only reported picture of John with his Mum Julia sat playing in the garden there. The Cadwallader's lived here for 62 years. The house was set next to a little park and the rear-faced the street. When John resurrected his music career in 1980, he talked of a family reunion at this address. John actually came back to Aunty Anne's house when he was famous on 26 June 1969 when he and Yoko, young Julian and Kyoko came to call, en route to Scotland. Aunty Anne died in December 1997.

Harriet (nee Stanley) Hafez, then Birch.- 1916 - 1973

Harriet was born in 1916 at 22 Huskisson Street, Liverpool (all the sisters' were born in different Stanley homes) She lived abroad for some years when she married an Egyptian, Ali Hafez (whom she met at Liverpool University) and they had a daughter Leila there. At the height of World War 2, Harriet and Leila return to United Kingdom by the quickest means possible. Declared as a "widow" and holding an Egyptian passport, she came back in 2nd class.

Harriet and daughter Leila stayed at Dairy Cottage, Woolton. Harriet later re-married Norman Birch- a garage manager from Woolton, becoming Harriet Birch. It was her new husband Norman who actually paid for Julia's funeral in 1958. John and his cousin Leila were close friends and had many childhood holidays together. Leila went to Calder Girls School near Quarry Bank School and was a star pupil later becoming an anaesthetist in Manchester. Years later, John bought Aunt Harriet and her husband Norman a home at 137 Gateacre Park Drive, where John stayed over in 1970 with Yoko and their kids. Harriet died in 1973.

Julia (nee Stanley) Lennon – 1914 – 1958

Mother of John Winston Lennon. The rest you probably know.

Chapter 3 - Paul McCartney's Family Tree (Paternal Side)

Just like John Lennon, there are many interesting and unexpected aspects to Paul McCartney's family tree too. All the Beatles had Irish emigrant roots, John had Welsh roots too and both Ringo, George and Paul also had roots from the Isle of Man. The Isle of Man connection for Paul in particular has provided some surprising information if my research is correct and as the story unfolds I'll clarify more unknown details of the McCartney clan.

1795 onwards

Great, Great, Great, Grandfather McCartney

James McCartney – Labourer Born 1795-- County Monaghan, Ireland
Catherine Cearns* – Wife   Born 1801 - County Tyrone, Ireland

Married 18 July 1820- St Peter's Church, Church Street Liverpool

*Catherine Cearns is misspelt on several documents as Carens

Siblings
Margaret- Born 1821 (Bap: St Mary's)
James (2) Born 1824 (Bap: St Mary's)* **(Paul McCartney's Great, Great, Grandfather)**
Mary   Born: 1825 (Bap: St Mary's)
John   Born 1828 –Died 1889 (Walton Workhouse)
Edward   Born 1832 (Bap: St Peter's Priory)
Catherine Born 1837 (Bap: St Peter's Priory)
James (3) Born 1839 (Bap: St Mary's) Died 1840
Joseph   Born 1840 Died 1846 (Bur: St Anthony's)

Child mortality was high during the 1800's. And it was not uncommon to use the name of a deceased child again. James McCartney born 1824 however, was alive in 1839 so it seems unusual for another child in the family to bear the name James whilst another was still alive.

In 1840 the McCartney family were living in Midghall Street, Vauxhall, Liverpool

1841 Census reports that the McCartney family had now moved to 7 Shawhill Street, Bradbury Court, Liverpool (Old Haymarket). James (1) was still a labourer and James (2) was an apprentice tailor.

1851 Census shows that the family remained at 7 Bradbury Court. James Senior (57) was still a labourer. James Junior had left home. John and Edward were also labourers. Mary and Catherine Junior were servants but living at home.

Days after the census was prepared James McCartney senior died aged 58. His address was quoted then as Preston Street, Old Haymarket (just around the corner from Shawhill Street). He was buried April 27 1851 at St Anthony's Church, Scotland Road, public grave 101 with 16 other people.

The 1861 census reveals that Catherine McCartney (widow) had now moved back out to Vauxhall district living in a tenement at 5 Charter Street. All her family had gone.

Catherine McCartney doesn't make a re-appearance on available records until 1873 showing up as a resident in another tenement in the Vauxhall district at 2 in 4 Court, Pall Mall, Vauxhall.

In 1876 Catherine McCartney died aged 75 and was buried on October 31 1876 at another pauper's cemetery Liverpool Parochial Cemetery- Walton, grave no: 1607.

The Children of James & Catherine McCartney

Son Edward McCartney born 1883. as a carter by trade and married late in 1881. In 1891 he was an "inmate" at Mount Pleasant Liverpool Workhouse (likely infirmary) and died in 1900.

Daughter Catherine McCartney married Thomas White in 1858. Lived at 72 Vernon Street, Liverpool most of her life and survived until at least 1896.

John McCartney born 1829 never married it seems. He worked as a salt heaver at the docks and lived in a boarding house. He died in 1889.

Daughter Mary McCartney born 1829 never married either and died around 1896.

Margaret McCartney born 1821 may have married around 1843 but nothing found so far.

The Life of James McCartney (2) 1824 - 1857

Great, Great, Grandfather McCartney

James McCartney (2) was born in Liverpool in 1824.
He married 14 July 1844 at St.Nicholas's Church, Liverpool.

Married- Rosanna Hughes (born 1825 –Ireland)
James McCartney declared as an upholsterer (minor- below 20)
Rosanna Hughes- (also a minor)- declared as a spinster.
Both living in Circus Street, Everton

Interestingly- the witnesses at the wedding was Bernard and Eliza McCartney suggesting more McCartney family came from Ireland besides James Senior at the same time.

Siblings:
James (4) Born 16 February 1845 (Bap: St Nicholas's) **(Paul McCartney's Great Grandfather)**
Anne   Born 1847   (Bap: St Mary's)
Francis   Born 1850   (Bap: St Nicholas's)
Joseph   Born 1858   (Bap: Holy Cross)

Note- The baptism for James (4) shows he was born 16 February 1845 indicating he was a pre-marital baby. Further note the witness at the baptism was Rosanna's brother, James Patrick Hughes, a plumber by trade.

For reasons unknown James McCartney (2) doesn't appear on the 1851 census records. His wife Rosanna (known as Rose) appears on the 1851 census living back with her parents, James and Alice Hughes. They were Irish and ran a provisions shop at 35 Hodson Street, Liverpool. She brought with her James (4) and Francis (10m old). It may be that daughter Anne died since last known.

Logic would suggest that either James went to work outside of Liverpool but he would show up elsewhere in the U,K on the day of the census. The other reasonable excuses are that maybe he worked at sea but his trade (upholsterer) makes that unlikely. The remaining thought is he served time in a workhouse i.e. the infirmary or even prison. I have scoured the prison and court registers and luckily nothing appears for James McCartney.

On 27 June 1857 James McCartney was buried at St.Oswald's Church, Old Swan, Liverpool. He had died at the Liverpool Workhouse, most likely at their infirmary after illness. The church confirms no memorial stone for James as was put in a mass grave.

In November 1857 Rosanna re-married whilst pregnant to her late husband's child. She married a John Andrew Templeton, a provision dealer like her father. They married at St Anthony's church and went to live at 39 Hodson Street in the Scotland Road district of Liverpool a few doors away from where her parents home and shop until recently.

Almost 9 months after James's death, Rosanna McCartney had her final child to him, Joseph, born 25 March 1858. This would suggest the death of James's was sudden and all the more tragic.

The 1861 census reports that Rosanna and John Templeton lived with young James McCartney now a plumber's apprentice, very probably working with his Uncle James Hughes. Rosanna (Rose) also had a new child John James Templeton aged 6 months and a 3 year old Joseph. There is no mention of Francis who died in 1852 at 20 months old and buried at St Anthony's Church. Her now widowed mother was living there too in the working class area, which was mostly slum housing and poor conditions to live in anyway which was proven when her 2nd husband John Templeton died aged 30 in 1867. He was buried at Ford Cemetery, Bootle.

With a young family and being only just 45 years old in July 1870 Rose Templeton re-married for the third time. She married an Irishman Patrick Needham, another provision dealer and they remained at 39 Hodson Street until Rose passed away in 1886. Her third husband Patrick passed away in 1905. They were buried together at Ford Cemetery, Bootle- No:362.

The children of James and Rosanna McCartney

Anne- born 1847 died 1847 (5m). Buried at St Anthony's
Francis- born 1850- died 1852- Buried in St Anthony's Church- mass grave
Joseph – born 1858 possibly died 1891. Buried at Toxteth Cemetery S7 No: 161
James   - born 1845- see next article.

Looking into the often brief history of the McCartney clan in this generation I noted the following interesting record.

Joseph McCartney signed up to the **Royal Navy** as an ordinary seaman (B2 rating) between 1874 and 1877. He served upon the following ships, H.M.S Caledonia, Impregnable, Ganges and R. Adelaide. He was however, discharged from the Royal Navy in 1877 following possible desertion (twice- once in 1874 aged 16 and aged 19 1877) and he spent 42 days in Bodmin Gaol, Cornwall for his supposed crime. Bodmin Gaol held prisoners of war as well as regular criminals. It also held public hangings and was the first British gaol to have separate cells for prisoners. It's now a hotel. The Royal Navy records for Joseph add a few more details of the man including his features, brown hair, hazel eyes , scar on left arm, ruddy complexion and height 5 feet 5 and half.

The Life of James McCartney (4) 1845- 1891

Great, Grandfather McCartney

The fourth James McCartney on record and the third James McCartney born in Liverpool. He married 1 November 1864 whilst still a minor (below 20 yo) at St.Peter's Church, Church Street, Liverpool.

James McCartney "minor" : Address Scotland Road. Profession : Plumber.
Elizabeth Williams "minor": Address Scotland Road. Spinster.

Elizabeth Williams was born in Canning Street, Birkenhead on 13 November 1846. Her parents were George Williams and Jane Williams (nee Woolfall). Her father was a boilermaker/journeyman and evidence of this was the family move to Heap in Lancashire in 1851 and then over to Arley Street, Liverpool in 1852. By the 1861 census Elizabeth was working as a 14 year old house servant for a family at 36 Lime Kiln Lane, Vauxhall, Liverpool. Aged 18, she married James McCartney in 1864 and they moved into 6 Bevington Street, Vauxhall a poor working class slum area of Liverpool.

On 23 November 1866 Joseph McCartney was born. He was baptised at St.Anthony's Church, 9 December 1866.

Joseph was Paul McCartney's Grandfather

The 1871 census shows that the family were still living at 6 Bevington Street, Vauxhall and that James was still a plumber but a few things had changed by the 1881 census.

The 1881 census indicated that the McCartney family had moved a few streets away to 3:1 Court 16 Beau Street, Vauxhall, Liverpool. Elizabeth McCartney was nominated "Head", Joseph was now 14 and a barber. (In later life Joseph quit that trade to work at Cope's Tobacco as a cutter). There were two more additions to the family too. Mary Elizabeth (born 1873) aged 8 and Annie (born 1879) aged 2. James McCartney wasn't shown on the 1881 census. Elizabeth simply stated "husband a seaman". It's not expected for a 36 year old married plumber to suddenly go to sea. It was usually the profession of young, single men. It was also not uncommon to quote "husband at sea" as a euphemism for a person in prison to avoid ignominy in the neighbourhood. I investigated this aspect quite thoroughly and didn't trace any local court appearances or prison records which cancels out one theory.

I finally managed to find James McCartney (4) on an Welsh 1871 census. It shows James McCartney from Liverpool aged about 26 (27 actually) as an able seaman working on the "United Kingdom" Steam Salvage Tug operating from the River Mersey but working in Caldy Island, Tenby, Pembrokeshire, Wales at the time of the census. The tug boat was part of a small fleet including The "United States" which were all-metal paddle tugs, only 144 feet long and 24 feet wide that moved large ships around the River Mersey or towed them elsewhere i.e. Wales. The tug boats were owned by The United Steam Tug Company, 9 Chapel Street, Liverpool. The tugs were staffed by 12 men, all local. There are numerous stories of steamers colliding with the tugs in the River Mersey. I queried the Welsh census and why James appeared on **two census reports in 1871**. The answer was that the Welsh census was completed on 25 March 1871 and the Liverpool census was completed 14 September 1871. When the 1881 census rolled around James had gone back out to sea but this time, no alternative census.

On 3rd March 1891 James McCartney (4) died aged 46 of a cerebral haemorrhage at Liverpool Royal Infirmary. His death certificate reports his address was 20 Holborn Street, Kensington, Liverpool. His occupation at this time was Journeyman /Painter so his last years may have involved travelling with his trade. He was buried at Ford Cemetery, Bootle Plot: B251 but I couldn't locate this grave site.

The 1891 census was completed just a few weeks after James's death. Elizabeth (widow) was aged 44. Her eldest son Joseph was now a tobacco grinder (at Cope's). Daughter Mary Elizabeth may have worked at Copes' also as she was declared as a cigar maker. Annie was a scholar and there were two more additions to the family, James (5) aged 8, born 1882 and Florence aged 2, born 1889.

On 14 May 1896 son Joseph McCartney – tobacconist (29 years) married Florence Clegg (Clague) spinster (21 years). She hailed from Wendell Street, Toxteth. They married at Christ Church, Kensington. Her father was a fishmonger called **Paul Clegg**. (Much more on this later).

In December 1896 Elizabeth (Williams) McCartney aged 50, re-married. She married Joseph Brewer (widower) a paver at Christ Church Parish Church, Kensington. They lived at 52 Wightman Street, Kensington, Liverpool.

The 1901 census reports that the Elizabeth & Joseph Brewer plus family had moved to 13 Woodbine Grove, West Derby. James McCartney (5) was now working and a tobacco machine feeder (at Cope's I suspect). Interestingly, daughter Florence was still at home aged 12 and Mary E appears to have left. And repeating history it seems that Elizabeth McCartney was pregnant when husband James died as she had another daughter Ada in August 1891 as she appears on the 1891 census aged 9 years old.

Life at sea seems to have tempted James McCartney (5) as he appears as a waiter/steward on the Cunard steamship "Saxonia" sailing from Liverpool to Queenstown (Ireland) and onto Boston in early 1903. There is only one record so far traced on his life at sea.

1910 second husband Joseph Brewer died aged 68. He is buried at Ford Cemetery Plot M127.

The 1911 census shows that Elizabeth Brewer was a widow (again) aged 64 living now at 53 Kilshaw Street, West Derby. James had remained and was a labourer at the Tobacco factory (Copes). Florence was 22 and worked as a dressmaker whilst Ada was a boxmaker. (Annie had left home by now.)

Elizabeth (Williams (McCartney) Brewer died June 1919 aged 72 and her address up to the date of her death was 3 Goth Street, West Derby. She wasn't buried with her husband but buried at nearby Anfield Cemetery, S7 Grave 959

The Children of James (4) and Elizabeth McCartney

Florence McCartney 1888 – 1974
Florence married in 1918 to Walter S Hills a house painter. She had three children and moved to 8 Kent House, Lune, Beckenham. She died in 1974 in Lewisham.

Mary Elizabeth McCartney 1873-1943
Married Thomas Cannon in 1892- a sailmaker. Lived at 8 Huxley Street, Clubmoor, Liverpool. They raised 9 children. Died 1943. Buried at Anfield Cemetery Private Grave S12 No: 157

Annie McCartney 1879-1956
Married 1898 to John Ormesher- a bricklayer. Lived at 1 Goth Street, West Derby. Raised 7 children. Lived at 34 Sutcliffe Street, Kensington. Died in Liverpool in 1956.

James McCartney (5) 1882 -1970
Married and lived at 106 Delamore Street, Kirkdale. He was a retired wharf labourer when he died. He is buried at Ford Cemetery Plot AS715

Ada McCartney 1891- 1926
Married Nicholas Proom in 1926. Was living at 3 Goth Street, West Derby (with her Mother). Ada died in 1929 at Yew Tree- Fazackerley Sanatorium. She was buried in a public grave at Anfield Cemetery S6 Grave 336

The Life of Joseph McCartney 1866 – 1927

Grandfather McCartney

Joseph McCartney married Florence Clegg (Clague) On 14 May 1896. They initially lived in 12 Daisy Grove, Liverpool 7 and later moved to 7 Greenside, Everton.

The 1901 census reported that Joe and Florence were living at 8 Fishguard Street, Everton district. Joe was a Tobacco Cutter. It took them a few years to begin a family but they gradually arrived.

Siblings
Joseph James: Born 25/12/1896 (Bap: Christ Church, Kensington)   Died 1898
John William: "Jack" Born 1898 (Bap: St Benedict, Everton)
Ann Alice: Born 1899 (Bap: 1899 St Chrysotum)   Died 1901
Edith Kathleen: Born 1901 (Bap: St Chrysotum, Everton)
James "Jim" : Born 1902 (Bap: St Benedict, Everton)

Jim was Paul McCartney's father

Florence Mildred "Millie": Born: 1904 (Bap: Emmanuel Church, Everton)
Annie: Born 1905 (Bap: Emmanuel Church, Everton)
Jane Virginia "Jin" : Born 1910 (Bap St. Benedict)

Joseph James McCartney is buried at West Derby Cemetery- Section 7 Plot 1761
Ann Alice McCartney is buried at West Derby Cemetery- Section 5 Plot 265

The 1901 census reported that Joe and Florence were living at 8 Fishguard Street, Everton district. Joe was a Tobacco Cutter. This census also included Joe's Mother-In-Law/Widow Jane Clegg aged 64 who came from the Isle of Man. More on her later.

The 1911 census showed the family had moved onto 3 Solva Street, Everton a larger home with 6 reported rooms. It also seems that Mother-in Law Jane Clegg had died interim.

Joseph McCartney (Grandfather) died in October 1927 aged just 60. He is buried in a purchased grave at Anfield Cemetery Section 15 NO: 526.

Florence McCartney (Grandmother) died May 1945. She was resident at 8 Cottesbrook Place, Liverpool at the time (Daughter Edith's home). She is buried with Joe McCartney at Anfield Cemetery in the same plot.

The Children of Joseph & Florence McCartney

Joseph James: Born 25/12/1896   Died 1898. Joseph James McCartney is buried at West Derby Cemetery- Section 7 Plot 1761

John "Jack" William McCartney: Born 1898. Died 1964. Gassed in WW1 leaving him with an affected larynx. He was later a Liverpool bus conductor then a rent collector and even played with Jim McCartney in his jazz band.

Ann Alice McCartney. Born 1899 . Sadly died in 1901. Ann Alice McCartney is buried at West Derby Cemetery- Section 5 Plot 265

Edith Kathleen McCartney. Born 1901. Married 1924 to William Alex Stapleton (storekeeper) They raised 2 daughters. Edith died in 1966. Was living at 11 Scargreen Avenue until 1966. Buried at Anfield Cemetery S12 No: 2653

Florence Mildred "Millie" McCartney. Born: 1904. Married 1927 to Albert Lalley Kendall (Cotton Brokers Clerk). Florence Kendall died in 1990 in Wirral.

Annie McCartney. Born 1905. Married 1927 to Albert Danher (a relative of Mary Mohin). Albert died in July 1942 and was buried at West Derby Cemetery S11 No: 331.Annie died in 1950 and probably laid to rest with Albert. Her son worked at Cotton Brokers- Hannay's. She lived at 184 Boaler Street, Liverpool.

Jane Virginia "Jin" McCartney. Born 1910. Married Henry Harris a builder/joiner. Henry ran a business and helped build the stage at the Cavern and refurbish Paul's home at "Rembrandt", Heswall, Wirral. Paul held his 21st birthday party at his Aunties' home in Huyton in 1964. Aunty "Jin" died in 1992. She got a name check mention in Paul's song "Let Em In".

James "Jim" : Born 1902. Profession Cotton Broker/Salesman. Married Mary Patricia Mohin in June 1941. Jim met Mary Mohin through her relative Albert Danher who was married to his sister Annie and lived at 11 Scargreen Avenue in 1939. Mary was a qualified midwife and later a health visitor on the new post-war Liverpool housing estates of Speke and Allerton. Raised 2 boys, Paul and Michael. .

Mary died 31 October 1956 at Northern Hospital, Leeds Street, Vauxhall, Liverpool.
Jim re-married in 1964 to Angela Williams (Nee Stopforth) from Hoylake, Wirral. Jim died in March 1976 and was cremated. His ashes were laid in Landican Cemetery flower beds, Woodchurch, Wirral.

Siblings
James Paul McCartney Born 1942- Walton Hospital, Liverpool (known as Paul)
Peter Michael McCartney Born 1944- Walton Hospital, Liverpool. (known as Mike)

And the rest you probably know.

The Isle of Man Connection

The Isle of Man is an island and self-governing dependency set in the Irish Sea between England (adjacent to Lancashire and Cumbria) and Northern Ireland. It covers an area of 570 km and nowadays has a population around 84,000 people. Just like Ireland at the time of the potato famine, it too had an extensive period of mass emigration of its people to England and beyond. In that mass of people leaving the Isle of Man included relatives of the Beatles and some Beatle-connected people with an Isle of Man connection too.

Eric Clague

Eric Clague is known to a lot of Beatle historians. He was the cadet policemen who ran over and accidentally killed Julia Lennon on 15 July 1958 as she crossed Menlove Avenue on her way home. The coroner's report for Julia Lennon was "misadventure". Eric lost his job and became a postman. He married in 1965 and remained in Liverpool. He himself died in 2020. He has an Isle of Man connection as his name Clague originates from there.

It so happens that Paul McCartney has Isle of Man roots too. His grandfather Joseph McCartney married Florence Clegg in 1863. Her parents were Paul and Jane Clegg and both came from the Isle of Man. **They were both born with the surname Clague** not Clegg. Paul Clague moved to Liverpool in approximately 1838 and he anglicised his surname to Clegg. As there is an Isle of Man connection and a surname connection I investigated the often speculated story that both Clagues' were possibly related.

Eric Clague's family Tree

Eric Clague- Born in Liverpool 1933. Died 2020   Occupation Policeman/Postman
Married- 1965: Pauline Regan

Father of Eric
Richard H Clague- Born in Liverpool 1905. Died 1997 Occupation : Postman
Married- 1931: Harriet Roberts

Father of Richard H Clague
Richard Clague- Born 1879 Abbey Home Farm, Ballahot, Malew, Isle of Man
Occupation: Able Seaman
Married- Liverpool 1904 : Mary Roberts
Lived at 23 Juno Street, Liverpool
Died: 1945

Father of Richard Clague
John Clague- Born 1831 Arbory, Rushen, Isle of Man
Occupation: Labourer
Died- Malew, Isle of Man – 1883

Father of John Clague
John Clague- Born 1806 Port St.Mary, Rushen, Isle of Man
Occupation: Agricultural Labourer

Chapter 4 - Paul McCartney's Isle of Man Family Tree

Now I'll summarise the Paul McCartney family tree originating from the Isle of Man and you can see whether you notice any connections.

Paul's father was James McCartney (1902-1976)
James McCartney was the son of Joseph McCartney (paternal grandfather) (1866-1923) and Florence Clegg (1874-1944).

Florence McCartney (nee Clegg) was the daughter of Paul and Jane Clegg and both were born in the Isle of Man. The family history needs a little detail but believe me, it's worth it.

Paul Clegg
Paul Clegg was born **Paul Clague**. He changed his surname when he came to England. He was born in 1815 in Arbory, Isle of Man.
His parents were Robert Clague (1774-1827) and Elizabeth Clague (nee Comish) (1783-1849). They lived in Malew, Arbory, Isle of Man.

Robert and Elizabeth had 5 children:
Robert: Born 1810
Elizabeth: Born 1811
Richard: Born 1813
Charles: Born 1814
Paul: Born 1815

Daughter Elizabeth married a farmer, Thomas Clague (no relation) in 1836 and they had 5 children- all born in Malew, Isle of Man.

Jane-   Born: 1838
Thomas -Born: 1839
Ann -   Born: 1840
John-   Born: 1843
Paul-   Born 1850
Catherine Born: 1856

NOTES:
I noticed that in Mike McCartney's excellent book, "Thank U Very Much" in the "Maclineage" section, he states that Jane Clague's father was a farmer named Thomas Clague.

The Arbory and Malew locations seems a common thread with Eric Clague's lineage and the McCartney/Clague lineage but no family names seems to connect over to one another so this seems to suggest it has no grounds for speculation anymore. Eric Clague and Paul McCartney are not related.

Meanwhile, a young Paul Clague left the Isle of Man around 1838 and moved to Liverpool. It's not clear why the surname change was necessary but Paul renamed himself Paul Clegg hereafter. He married 3 times- all in Liverpool.

August 1840- Married Ann Bell (1819-1847) at St.Augustine Church, Everton
He declared his occupation as "wheelwright"
They had 4 children:
Thomas (1841), William (1843), Margaret (1844), Elizabeth (1845)

January 1849- Married Margaret Bell (1823-1856) St Nicholas's Church, Liverpool
He declared his occupation as "pattern-maker" this time.
They had 2 children: Ann Alice (1852) and Paul (1855)

Both marriage certificates report that Ann Bell's father and Margaret Bell's father (Thomas) was a watchcase maker by trade. They were in fact, the same father. So Paul Clegg married Ann **and then her sister**.

The 1851 census for Jane Clague (b. 1838) shows that at 13 years old she was a servant for the Gelling family in Malew, Isle of Man.

The 1861 census shows that 23 year old Jane Clague had now left the Isle of Man and was working as a servant at 33 Slater Street, Liverpool for a fishmonger, Paul Clegg who had a stall at 21 St John's Market.

September 1863 Paul Clegg and Jane Clague married. They had 2 children:
Gilbert Cummins Clegg (1869) and Florence (1874).

From the research I've made and the lineage sources I've checked, it appears that Jane Clague was possibly the daughter of Paul Clegg's own sister Elizabeth. Therefore Paul Clegg was in fact, the Uncle of Jane Clague and she was his niece. Marrying one's niece or nephew is known as an avunculate marriage and is said not to be permitted in the United Kingdom but it is permitted in countries including Australia, Canada and the U.S.A. I'd appreciate any further researchers to check over these details and see what they find.

Paul Clegg died in 1879 and is buried at Anfield Cemetery C of E section Section:2 No: 1124 (not found). I gather that Jane is buried with him.

Son Gilbert Cummins Clegg married in 1891 and was a dock labourer all his working life. He died in 1941 and is also buried at Anfield Cemetery Section 7 No: 1933.

Daughter and paternal grandmother of Paul McCartney, Florence Clegg went on to marry Joe McCartney and she died in 1944. The rest you probably know.

The Children of Paul Clegg (with Ann Bell and Margaret Bell)

Ann:
Thomas Bell Clegg. Born 1841. Died 1864 in Liverpool. Was a sailmaker by trade
Elizabeth Clegg. Born 1845. Married 1872 (Gibson). Was a milliner by trade. Died 1932 in Liverpool.
William Paul Clegg. Born 1843. Details unknown.

Margaret:
Anne Alice (Amelia) Clegg: Born 1852. Married 1878 (Gainham) Shopkeeper/Grocer by trade.
Paul Clegg (2) Born: 1855. Fishmonger by trade. Died 1900
Margaret (2) Born: 1844. Married 1868 (Lenham) Died 1921 in Liverpool.

Chapter 5 - Paul McCartney's Family Tree (Maternal Side)

Paul has strong Irish roots on his mother's (Mohin) side and just like his McCartney family roots, they originate from County Monaghan, Ireland. As I've found looking at Irish records of births, deaths and marriages, they are fairly random if they exist at all. The Irish census system only began in 1901 and any other consistent governmental records tend to be petty session court reports and dog licenses of all things. Here's what I've found.

The Mohin Family Tree

Paul McCartney was born in 1942, Walton, Liverpool, the first of two boys born to parents James McCartney and Mary Patricia McCartney (nee Mohin).

Mary Patricia Mohin was born in 1909 in Fazakerley, Liverpool. She had brothers, Wilfred Leo Mohin (1908 1981), Owen Michael "Bill" Mohin (1917-1970) and a sister, Agnes Mary Mohin (1915-1918).

Mary's parents were Owen Mohin (1880-) and Mary Theresa Mohin (nee Danher) (1877-1919) from Liverpool. Owen's surname has been changed from Mohan and prior to that it was Moan. Owen was born in Tullynamroe/Tullnamalra Ballycastle, County Monaghan, Ireland. Owen came from Ireland and when he left home he initially lived in Scotland firstly working as a coal merchant/hawker, living at 9 MacIntyre Street, Glasgow. He married Mary Theresa Danher in April 1905 in Liverpool and raised 4 children, losing daughter Agnes when she was just 3 years old.

Owen Mohin's parents were Owen Moan (1840-1903) a farmer from Tullnamalra/Tullynamra, County Monaghan and Mary Moan (nee McGeogh) (1847-1923). They married in 1876 in Castleblayne, County Monaghan, Ireland. They had at least 7 children.

I mentioned earlier that Irish ancestry records are thin on the ground but there appears to be a large presence of McGeogh's from the Castleblayne area as a number of McGeoghs' appear in the Petty Session Courts for notable things like fence stealing, assault and drunkenness. There is an interesting Petty Session record for a "Owen Moan" from Tullynamalro in June 1870, accusing this person of holding a quantity of blasting powder in his house, contrary to the statute. Imagine.! Just to add contrast, another official record held for an "Owen Moan" is his registration for a dog license in 1902 to record that he owned a small terrier.

Owen Moan's father was a Michael Moan (farmer) presumably from the same parish in Castleblayne but there the trail dries up. Whereas Mary McGough's father was a Michael McGeogh (1810-1871), a farmer also who came from Drumgarra and after that her family line records dry up too.

The Danher Family Tree

Mary McCartney's own mother Mary Theresa Danher was born in Liverpool. Her parents were John Danher (1842-1917) and Jane Baines (1848-1920). John was from Limerick City, Ireland. Jane came from Dudley, Worcestershire. The family settled in Liverpool 1873/84 but not before firstly living in Middlesbrough, Ireland and then Bradford where several children were registered as born. They raised at least 10 children.

John Danher was a gas meter maker around 1881, living at 23 Holt Road, West Derby and moving onto 43 Holt Road West Derby at around 1891 but then onto 98 Aigburth Road, Toxteth Park in 1901 when it was shown he running a tallow (for candles and soap) and chandler shop with his family.

In 1911 John had retired and now lived with his wife and daughters across the River Mersey to a nice home (still there) at 58 Leasowe Road, Wallasey. John Danher died in 1917 and his wife Jane died in 1920 at the same address. They were buried back in Liverpool at Yew Tree Cemetery, West Derby Plot 4A/167 with their daughters Sarah Rebecca and Winifred Ruth.

In 1956 Paul McCartney's mother died and she was buried in Yew Tree Cemetery Plot 3A/276 with her step-mother (Rose) which should include her father but he is buried in the same cemetery elsewhere. This plot is famously vacant of a gravestone. Mike McCartney's book "Thank U Very Much" says his mother is buried with her mum Mary Theresa and sisters so I'd surmise plot 4A/167 may be her actual resting place.

The Baines Family Tree

Jane Danher (1848-1920) was born Jane Baines in Dudley, Worcestershire. Her father John Baines (1823-1900) was an innkeeper. His wife was Elizabeth Cook (1823-1864) and in 1861 they lived in Birmingham city centre at Cregoe Street. They moved to Durham in later years where John became a tailor by way of a complete change of job. When Elizabeth died in 1864, he re-married a brief while later and then moved onto Middlesbrough.

John Baines parents were Frederick and Elizabeth Baines. Frederick (1803-1865) was born in St.Martin's, Worcestershire and this is where, by coincidence, the Woolam strand of George Harrison's family came from.

Chapter 6- George Harrison's Family Tree

Once you've read through George's family tree you'll see that like his band mates, how varied and mixed his family background was, notably that his ancestors came from all over the United Kingdom and Ireland. True to all the Beatle families and history there was a lot of family tragedy. Many children died young and many ancestors lost their husband or wives (often very early on) but often they re-married and carried on. If it had not been for these sad losses and often painful changes of circumstances things may not have turned out like they did.

Irish Roots of George Harrison

George's mother had an English mother, Louise Woollam and Irish father, John French. John was born in 1870 and came to England from County Wexford, Ireland in his late twenties. The French surname (also stated as Ffrench) is a relatively rare surname found in Ireland. The name originated in France (where else) and was brought over by the Normans who landed in Bannow Bay, County Wexford, Ireland in 1169. They became land owners and prospered but following Oliver Cromwell's regime and notably The Sack of Wexford in 1649, the Roman Catholic Ffrench families had their land confiscated and from that point on, they became impoverished farmers or labourers working for the new Protestant land owners.

The earliest record of a recognised member in George Harrison's Irish family is Michael French born 1800. He married Elizabeth Kennedy born 1804 and was probably married before 1820. They had one child found on record.

James Darby French- born 1825- Ballyoughter, County Wexford.

I'm not able to figure what the middle name is in reference to yet.

I can't go back further than Michael French as yet either though I did establish Elizabeth Kennedy was the daughter of John Kennedy and Mary Graham and she was born in Killaveny, Ballinamanogue, County Wexford in 1805. John Kennedy was born in 1770 in Ferns, County Wexford (You'll see a lot of French surnames in the Ferns area). His parents were John Kennedy and Margaret Smith.

Michael French later shows up on land reports/valuations around 1854 as the land occupant/farmer of 1 acre in St.John's, Forth, County Wexford (Enniscorthy) value £3.

Michael French died in 1880 and his wife Elizabeth died in 1875 and is probably buried in one of the churches in Enniscorthy. Michael may be possibly buried at Selskar Abbey grave 33.

Their son, James Darby French remained in County Wexford and moved to Ballycarney, Ferns, County Wexford. He married Ellen Whelan in 1857. Ellen Whelan lived at Corah, near Ballycarney, County Wexford. Ellen was the daughter of James Whelan and Catherine Kinsella. Corah was a slated dwelling house with a cow shed, piggeries and a fowl house and after the death of James (1907) and Ellen (1906) and daughter Eliza (1911) it was auctioned off in 1913.

The couple raised 6 children. Catherine (1863 -1863 (Buried at Selkskar Abbey Grave 20), Eliza, Mary, James, Denis (1873) and John (Born 1870- Ballycarney). It was John French who left Ireland and moved to Liverpool and was **George Harrison's maternal grandfather**.

James Darby French and Ellen French remained at Corah, farming 2 acres of land and suffering great hardship and poverty.

The few Irish records that can be found include Petty Sessions- Court reports usually over small unlawful acts in the local towns. A number of records show a person named as Ellen French attending nearby Enniscorthy court to either make a complaint about a crime or even be the named defendant of a crime. I found records from 1856 up to 1894 showing an "Ellen French" as the victim of assault, not licensed to sell spirits, stealing, being stolen from and more. No more can be found to establish if this is John Derby's wife or not but she was quite a character if it was her.

Only the 1901 Irish census is on record. It shows that James French was living at Corah, Tombrack, County Wexford. He was an agricultural labourer and a Roman Catholic. His wife Ellen was still alive and their daughter Eliza was the only child remaining home.

Eliza married in 1908 (to Patrick Murphy) but sadly died in 1911 in Enniscorthy. Brother Denis went to live in West Dublin. He became a bread van driver living at Daniel Street, Wood Quay Dublin and later a labourer living at 83 Harold's Cross Cottages, Rathmines, West Dublin. Sister Mary and brother James whereabouts are unknown.

James Darby French died 1907 and his wife Ellen died in 1906. Burial details are not known yet.

Son John French left for England in late 1890's. He was on the 1901 U.K. census as a barman working at the Black Horse pub/hotel, Little Heswall, Wirral. There's also been some hints that he worked as a commissionaire at the New Brighton Tower Ballroom (known as New Brighton Tower & Recreation Co. Ltd – run by Albert Bulmer, 5 Virginia Road, New Brighton). The Ballroom was a grand building set on the coast of Wallasey facing the then busy River Mersey and across from that was the bustling city of Liverpool. New Brighton was a pleasant Victorian coastal resort with beaches, open air swimming pools, funfairs and promenades and thousands flocked to it from Birkenhead and Liverpool and further afield for day trips and holidays. The Tower Ballroom features some 60 years later when the Beatles played there many times. The Tower Ballroom was officially opened in 1898/1900 so if John French worked there that would place him living locally at the time. Lower Heswall is a nice hamlet a short distance away in the Wirral Peninsula. There is a photograph of John French handling a horse carriage for the Black Horse pub and it's believed he transported customers to the ferry and boats moored on the River Mersey which was some miles away at Woodside in Birkenhead. As he did so, there's a high chance this is where and how he met his future wife Louise Woolam. Louise was working as a maid at the Ranelagh Hotel, 86 Chester Street, Birkenhead, very close to the Mersey ferries terminus at Woodside. The Ranelagh Hotel was handy for the Mersey Ferry over the River Mersey and the transatlantic ships leaving Liverpool daily.

John French and Louise Woolam

The first indication that John and Louise were a couple appears on the 1911 census. They are living at 11 Albert Grove, Wavertree, South Liverpool. John is now working for the Liverpool Corporation (Council) as a street lamplighter. He reports on the census form that they have been married 7 years. Truth is, they never officially married so this is more likely how long they had been together- since about 1904. They also had several children at this time.

Kathleen Ellen French: born 1905- Liverpool
Mary Elizabeth French: born 1908- Liverpool
John French: born 1909- Liverpool
Louise French: born 1911 (1 month old) Liverpool

Louise was George Harrison's mother.

John and Louise French only ever moved one more time in their lives, all the way to 9 Albert Grove, Wavertree as later Electoral Roll records show.

By 1919 it was known that John French had become a policeman/constable as he was involved in the "Liverpool Lock Out" in August 1919 and went on strike for better pay and conditions. John was a regular policemen working for Liverpool City Police. It was a hard job, six days a week, long hours, rough neighbourhoods and often rest days were lost due to court case appearances. The pay was lower than the dock workers' and promotion often went to staff not on the beat. It was also alleged that the police force was rife with secret societies and organisations too. A union leader and police sergeant called Robert Tissyman, originally a miner from South Hutton, Durham helped organise the Liverpool strike of policemen and of the 1824 policeman on the force, 954 went on strike including John French. The result of the strike was an expected surge in crime, looting of shops, 1 death and a lot of rioting. The army fixed bayonets and stood outside shops in London Road, There were baton charges on rioters. A tank was parked in readiness at St. George's plateau and the naval warship HMS Valiant was in the River Mersey just in case matters worsened. The strike ended a few days later and those who striked were not hired back with no rights of appeal, including John French. Liverpool City Police rather unwisely advertised for replacement policemen and ended up having criminals joining and burgling properties themselves. Robert Tissyman, who lived at 37 Albert Edward Road, went to the Court Assizes at St George's Hall in September for his part in the strike, found guilty of unlawful assembly and jailed for 1 day. He quit the force and became an insurance agent. There is a picture of John French as a policeman in that era and it's quite uncanny how much he resembles his grandson (and vice versa) in George's 1967 persona.

As for where John French worked as policeman. He lived at 11 Albert Grove, Wavertree and literally a 100 yards away was Wavertree Police Station at 63-69 High Street, Wavertree. It's still there today. If it wasn't this branch he worked from then it was the larger Liverpool City Police station at 106-114 Lawrence Road, Wavertree just over a mile away (still there). As Robert Tissyman lived nearby too, I suspect John and Robert worked at the same station or at least knew each other.

It's not yet known what John French did in the years after 1919 to his death in 1937. He remained at 9 Albert Grove, Wavertree with wife Louise. At one time in 1936/37, George French lived there with them. There was a George French from home town Enniscorthy, Ireland, a plumber by trade and he may well have been a cousin visiting.

John French died in January 1937 and was buried in Allerton Cemetery-private grave S17 No: 477

Widow Louise French remained at 9 Albert Grove, Wavertree for the rest of her life. Her granddaughter Louise Harrison lived in the next road at 12 Arnold Grove. Her daughter Mary Fox lived a few doors away to be replaced by other Fox relatives at 12 Albert Grove. The 1939 register shows that Louise French now had a job as a library cleaner. This may very well be Wavertree Library situated just a few yards away on High Street, Wavertree. Louise French saw all of Louise Harrison's family grow up, including George.

The children of John French and Louise (Woolam) French

Kathleen Ellen French born 1905- died 1995

Married in 1928 to William J Phillipson who was a clothing club collector. They lived at 11 Everest Road, Tranmere, Birkenhead for a while. She returned to Liverpool some time later and she died at St.Joseph's Home, Woolton Road, Liverpool in January 1995. She is buried at Allerton Cemetery RC Section S15 No: 182

Mary Elizabeth French – born 1908- Died 2005.
Married Edward Fox in 1934. Lived at 12 Albert Grove for some time and then her Fox relatives (Francis and Alice) moved in. She raised 2 children. She last resided at The Lodge, Yewfield, Archbishop House, Church Rd. Woolton and died in 1962.

John French (2) Born 1909- Died 1968
Married Elizabeth Casson in Liverpool in 1938. Last known living at 83A Woolton Road, Garston (above a fruit shop). Died 1968 and buried with his parents at Allerton Cemetery S 17 No: 477.

Louise French (2) Born 1911- Died 1970
Married Harold Hargreaves Harrison (1909- 1978). Raised 4 children, Peter, Harold (2), Louise and George. **George Harrison's mother** .

Chapter 7 - The Woolam Family Tree

Firstly, the problem with archive records and recorders. If the names are unusual, they invariably are spelt different ways by census writers and clergy et al. Illiteracy amongst working class folk of the 1800's and early 1900's also meant they may not have known how to spell their own name and they could only muster an "X" on marriage certificates for a signature. The Woolam name is no exception as it appears in several guises, Woolam, Woollam, Wullum, Wollam. I'll use Woolam throughout. So now you know.

Louise Woolam was born in 1879 in Little Crosby, North Liverpool, Lancashire.

The earliest Woolam relative found is James Woolam from Whixall, Prees, near St.Martins, Shropshire (Salop). He was married to Ann Willams in 1776. Their son Charles Woolam was born 1778 in Whixhall, Shropshire. He married Elizabeth Jones in 1806 and they had a son Roger Woolam born in 1810 and he was baptised in Llanymynech, St.Martins, St.Asaph Diocese (Wales). Roger married Ann Swallow born in 1811 (daughter of John Swallow and Benedicta Edwards). Anne probably came from Dyffryn Aled, near Presatatyn, North Wales. Their marriage in 1835 was in the Denbighshire area most likely. They had a son, John Woolam in 1838.

John Woolam next appears aged 4 living in Claypit Street, Whitchurch, Shropshire. There's no indication that his co-residents are relatives.

The 1851 census finds John Woolam living at The Old Shop, St.Martins, Shropshire and he's back with the Woolam family including 3 other children. His father Roger's occupation is gardener/agricultural labourer and John was a farmer's servant.

In 1861 John had left Shropshire and was living as a boarder at Quarry Farm, Appleton, Parish of Farnworth, Warrington, Cheshire. (Harry and Louise Harrison later moved out to Appleton in the mid 1960's). John was working as a gardener himself now.

He married in 1862. He was living in South Street, Dingle (set at the bottom of Madryn Street where Ringo was born). His bride was Isabella Flanagan from Heath Street, Toxteth. They married in Toxteth at St Michael in the Hamlet. They moved up to the cleaner air and spaces of Little Crosby and raised 1 child, Margaret. Sadly, Isabella died in 1866.

The 1871 census reports that widower John was now living at, The Lodge, Little Crosby Hall as a gardener. He had a son, John (5) and daughter, Margaret (7). Its possible Isabella died in childbirth. In addition, the family had a general servant; Lydia Daniels aged 16 so they were prosperous enough to afford help.

In November 1872 John Woolam re-married. He married Jane Daniels (born 1850) aged 22 from Farnworth and was most likely a relative of his own house servant, Lydia.

By the 1881 census the Woolam family had moved to 1 Virgin's Lane, Little Crosby. They now had three more children, George, Walter and **Louise**.

In November 1890 John Woolam died aged 55. He was buried by Rev. J C Fred Brindley at St Helen Church, Bridge Lane, Sefton, Lancashire. His estate was reported at £20.

Without John's wage the family had to change. Widowed Jane Woolam moved to live at 3 Victoria Road, Little Crosby and worked as a dressmaker with her 11 year old daughter, Louise was still a scholar.

Widow Jane Woolam came from Farnworth, Widnes where John had a worked a brief while. Her parents were James and Mary Anne Daniels. James Daniels worked in the local industry, chemical works as an alkali labourer. The area produced caustic soda, bleach powder and similar products. The Daniels family lived in Bog Lane, Farnworth. Jane had one brother, John and a sister, Esther.

Her 1861 census report is interesting. Aged 11 she is recorded as a "nurse". The 1871 census then states she is living at home still and a servant. By 1872 she had married.

Jane Woolam (nee Daniels) re-married in 1891. She married a mason/builder called William Collins from Barnstaple, Devon. The 1901 census shows they re-located to live at Hilbre Road, West Kirby, Wirral. On this record it appears that her brother Walter came to live with them. He too was a mason.

The 1911 census shows that Jane had become a widow in the interim. She was now living back in Liverpool at 30 Sampson Street, Everton with her brother Walter in tow, now unemployed.

In 1918 Jane Collins (nee Daniels/Woolam) died. She had last resided at 222 Rathbone Street, West Derby and was buried in a pauper's grave in Everton Cemetery Section3 No: 339.

Her brother Walter may have fallen on hard times or an illness as he next went to live at 9 Albert Grove with his sister's mother-in-law, Louise French. He died in 1934 and was buried in Everton Cemetery too, public grave S13 No:283.

Chapter 8- The Harrison Family Tree

The eighteenth century is where you can find the earliest record of the Harrison family tree.

I firstly found a birth record of Robert Harrison born 29 September 1771 in Prescot/Whiston. His father is shown as Edward Harrison-farmer and his mother was Ann.

Robert Harrison was a farmer in Prescot, Lancashire. He married Sarah Orrett/Orret in 1794. Sarah Orret was born in 1770 in Rainford, Lancashire. They appear to have at least 3 children, Anthony (1797), Ralph (1799) and Martha (1800).

Anthony Harrison was George Harrison's Great, Great, Great Grandfather (1797– 1863)

Anthony was a joiner by trade. He married in December 1816 at St.James Church, Walton on the Hill, Liverpool to Elizabeth Orrett. I can't establish what relative, if any, Elizabeth was to Sarah Orrett.

Before the first official census was launched in 1841 the couple had three children.
Robert (2): born 1816- West Derby (became a joiner)
Ann: born 1832
Ralph: born.?

The 1841 census shows that Anthony and Elizabeth had settled in Town Row, West Derby, Liverpool. He was a joiner still. They had 7 children this far. Martha, Anthony (2)- a joiner, Ralph, Ann, Mary , Susannah, Sarah (2). They have a number of farm labourers, blacksmiths and the like living in Town Row which may have been a rural area of agricultural farm land.

When the 1851 census was completed, the family had more additions. Another son, Henry appears. Henry was aged 23 and was a bricksetter/layer so he may have been working away as journeymen did in 1841. The Harrison family also acquired granddaughter Margaret on the census. They remained at Town Row, West Derby. Martha, Sarah(2), Ann and Mary were all laundresses.

The 1861 census reported that the Harrison clan had now moved to Deys Lane, West Derby, Liverpool.. Anthony was now a house carpenter and a widower. Elizabeth died in 1866. Daughters Martha, Ann and Margaret were still living with him plus a previously undisclosed son, William aged 12. They also had in residence a number of grandchildren. Ralph, Walter, William, Margaret, Susannah, Elizabeth and Emma.

In June 1863 Anthony Harrison died and was buried in Huyton Parish.

Robert Harrison (2) was George Harrison's Great, Great Grandfather (1816 – 1877)

Robert married Jane Shepherd (1816- Litherland) in November 1835 at St.Nicholas's Church, Liverpool

His 1841 census reports that he lived at 32 Prescot Road, Kensington, Liverpool. He was a joiner by trade and by now had three children, Alice (1837), Anthony (2) (1840) and Mary (1841).

The 1851 census showed no change of address. The work was plentiful in Liverpool for artisans like Robert and many exquisite well-built grand houses in the Liverpool area were built and remain there today. The family had enlarged to include Elizabeth, Robert (3) and **Edward (1848)**. Notwithstanding a big family they also had mother-in-law Mary Shepherd and brother-in-law William living there too. Daughter Alice (14) was oddly living with her Uncle Edward Shepherd in West Derby Village in 1851.

The 1861 census shows prosperity in the Robert Harrison family. He was now an employer of 1 man and 1 boy as joiners. They still lived in Prescot Road and they had more children. William, Jane, Esther and Margaret.

The family had moved along Prescot Road by the next census. The 1861 census indicates a move to 44 Prescot Road. Robert was still a joiner. Son James was a bricklayer and son Robert was also a joiner. Things didn't change greatly on the 1877 census in this respect but his mother-in-law returned and a grandson John was in residence now.

In 1877 Robert Harrison died.

The 1881 census showed a change in fortune following the loss of Robert. Jane Harrison was now a widow and had moved to 19 Derby Street, West Derby. She was living with her brother again and her now married daughter Jane (Robinson) and her daughter Alice.

In 1888 Jane Harrison died

Edward Harrison was George Harrison's Great Grandfather (1848- 1925)

Edward was born in 1848. He was a stonemason by trade. He married Elizabeth Hargreaves in May 1868. He was living in Gill Street, Liverpool at the time. Elizabeth was born in 1850 and was brought up at 9 Holgate Street, Manchester until she moved to Pembroke Place, Liverpool not far from Gill Street.

The 1871 census shows the couple were living in Mary Adelaide Place, Old Swan, Liverpool and had already had 2 children. Mary Ann (1869) and Robert (1871).

By the 1881 census the family had moved to 14 Queen Street, West Derby, Liverpool. There were more children in the fold too. Elizabeth, Robert (3), Jane.

The 1891 census had shown some changes. Still living at 12 Queen Street. Son Robert was a stonecutter, William a bricklayer. More additions to the family included (Henry (1882) Joseph (1884) and George (1886). **Henry would be George Harrison's grandfather**.

The new century and the 1901 census updated Edward Harrison's family. Edward was now a bricklayer, as was Henry and other brother Joseph. Brother George was a roper. There were even more additions to the family with the arrival of Harold aged 8 and Richard aged 5. Richard appears to have been born in Salford. Possibly due to a family residence with the Mancunian branch of the family.

The 1911 census revealed that Edward and Elizabeth now only had son Richard- now a labourer, living at home plus grandson William.

There were a number of family tragedies and incidents in the forthcoming years and WW1 played it's part. In 1920 Elizabeth Harrison passed away, In 1915 their youngest son Richard Hargreaves Harrison went to war (a machine gunner/private in the army). He was disabled off with an army pension but thankfully, lived on until 1980. It was son, Henry Harrison who proved to be the greatest loss.

Henry Harrison – Grandfather to George Harrison (1882 – 1915)

In 1902, bricklayer Henry Harrison married Jane Thompson at Holy Trinity Church, Wavertree.

Jane was a local girl born in 1885. She lived at 16 Wellington Road, Wavertree. Her father James was a railways linesman/engine driver who came from Kirkinnner, Wigtownshire, Scotland the son of Archibald Cunningham who was a train driver who came to Liverpool with his family. James' wife Annie came from Ramsay, Isle of Man. Jane had three sisters and one brother. Jane was a baker's assistant in a confectioners.

According to the 1911 census Henry and Jane were living at 31 Wellington Grove, Wavertree and had raised 4 children, Elizabeth (1903), Henry (1905), Edward (1907) and Harold (1909). **Harold was George Harrison's father**. Other family followed from 1911 to April 1915. James (1911), William (1913) and Jane (April 1915).

When WW1 began Henry Harrison joined the fight. In November 1914 he was made a private soldier in the 1st Battalion, Loyal North Lancs Regiment (Service No: 18190). Very sadly he was killed on the first day of the Battle of Loos 25 September 1915. His wife Jane received the news of his death 1 month later at her next address, 24 Abyssinia Street. Later Jane began to received a war gratuity. Henry was buried at St.Mary's Advanced Dressing Station Cemetery, Haisnes, Dept du pas de Calais, France plot VF10. His youngest daughter Jane never saw him.

Jane Harrison died aged 35 in 1919 and is possibly buried in Toxteth Park Cemetery.

Harold Harrison – Father of George Harrison (1909 – 1978)

As a young man Harold had a number of jobs in Liverpool before trying his hand as a ship steward on the liners. It was around then in 1931 that he married Louise French. The 1939 register shows he quit the liners in preference to becoming a bus conductor on the corporation buses and later progressing to being a bus driver which he did until he retired. His first marital home was a small 2-up 2 down council house at 12 Arnold Grove, Wavertree. Luckily he had a lot of relatives in the neighbourhood.

Harold and Louise brought up 4 children. Louise (2) born 1931, Harold James (2) (1934), Peter Henry (1940) and George (1943).

The family lived in several council houses in Speke and Wavertree after leaving Arnold Grove in George's early childhood. Following George's fame and fortune as a Beatle, he bought his parents a home in Appleton, Warrington. Louise (nee French) Harrison died in 1970 and Harold Hargreaves Harrison died in 1978. They were both cremated at Walton Lea Crematorium, Warrington.

The rest you probably know.

Chapter 9 - Ringo Starr's Family Tree

It's not uncommon to find Ringo being featured last of all in most Beatle books but his life story and family tree are quite dramatic and certainly needs telling just as much as the others.

I approached Ringo's family tree from two aspects. One is the Gleave family strand and other is the more mysterious and quite tragic Starkey story. After all, his true surname is **Parkin** and I found the origin of this change. There's also the Irish family connection which has always seemed less well established than his band mates and this review has put that to rights and may surprise you in the bargain.

The Gleave Family Tree

Gleave is the maiden name of Ringo's mother, Elsie.

The earliest record of a Gleave occurs on the marriage certificate in 1863 of William Gleave when he married Mary Openshaw. He stated his occupation as boilermaker and his father's name as Peter Gleave but the trail before that goes cold.

William Gleave and wife Mary's son William (2) born 1860 who was also a boilermaker married Mary Kate Conroy in Liverpool in 1889. The raised 5 children, William (1890), John (1891), Anne (1893) Ellen (1895) and James (1899).

Mary Catherine "Kate" Conroy was a Liverpool girl from a large family herself. Her parents were Mary Jane O'Connor and William Conroy. William, born 1835 was shown as an engine driver on the couple's marriage certificate. He reports that he came from Ireland but no more is known. Mary Kate Gleave died in 1916 and is buried at Ford R.C Cemetery, Bootle Plot K211. Husband William Gleave died in 1934, gravesite unknown.

Son John Gleave, yet another boilermaker was born in 1891 and married in 1914. He married Catherine Martha Johnson also born in 1891. **These were Ringo's maternal grandparents.**

Catherine Martha Johnson was known as "Kitty". Her father Andrew Johnson was a "flatman" and operated on flat bottomed, shallow water boats. He was a mariner but not a seagoing one therefore. He was born in 1852 in Delting, Shetland, in farthest Scotland. He came to Liverpool and in 1875 married Mary Elizabeth Cunningham (born 1858). They raised 6 children. Mary, Phillis, Elizabeth, Whilhemina, Andrew and Nancy.

Peter's own father, also called Peter, was a "mariner" too but he remained in Shetland. He wife Phillis (nee Tait) came from nearby Lunnasting, Shetland. They had 4 children, Mary, Ursula, Catherine and Peter (2). It was Peter (2) who left for Liverpool. Phillip's grandfather was Magnus Johnson born in 1771 and he married Ursula Jameson born in 1788. Magnus was a farmer in Shetland.

It was said that Mary Elizabeth Cunningham's father James was a gardener by occupation and hailed from County Mayo, Ireland. An 1881 census reports James Cunningham- gardener living at 64 Cressington Park, Garston and his birthplace was "Ireland". That may be, but I had no luck confirming his birthplace in Ireland but his wife Elizabeth lived with John & Kitty in 1891 and declared on that census that she came from Restrevor, Newry, Northern Ireland. Mother in law Elizabeth Cunningham died in 1911 and is buried at Toxteth Park Cemetery, SF left Grave 458. Andrew Johnson died in 1927 and was buried in Toxteth Cemetery D Left 474. His wife Mary Elizabeth Johnson died in 1931 and is buried with him.

Kitty and John Gleave raised 7 children which included a set of twins. Sadly three of them died young. The children were **Elsie (1914)**, Catherine (1916), Evelyn (1917), John & William (1919), William James (1920), Henry (1925) and Dorothy (1927).

John Gleave died in 1936 and Catherine "Kitty" died in 1966. They are buried together in Allerton Cemetery CH35 NO: 704.

Eldest daughter Elsie married Richard Henry Starkey- a baker in 1938 and raised one child Richard (Ringo) but the marriage broke up and Richard Henry Starkey left in 1943 to later live in Crewe.

In 1946 Harry Graves (born 1913) from Romford, London came to work in Dingle, Liverpool and soon started dating Elsie. They married in 1953 and raised step-son Richard "Ringo" Starkey. Elsie Graves (nee Gleaves/Starkey) died in 1987 and Harry Graves died in 1994.

Ringo's father, Richard Senior moved away to Crewe in Cheshire and remarried in 1954 to **Margaret Clarke**. He had no contact with the family thereafter and reportedly became a window cleaner. He died on 5 December 1981 and is buried in Middlewich Cemetery, Cheshire East Unitary, leaving an estate of £25000. Richard Henry Starkey's lineage is explained in great detail in the Starkey Story coming up but he needs a mention at this stage first. Richard Henry Starkey was the son of John Parkin Starkey and Annie Bower- born 1889. They brought up four children: John A Starkey, May Starkey (who died as a child), Nancy Starkey, (known as "Ann") and Richard Henry Starkey (**Ringo's father**).

The Bower Family Tree

Annie Bower was the daughter of Alfred (Born 1852) and Margaret Ellen Parr (Born 1855) who married in 1873. Like the Gleave clan, the Bower clan were a succession of metal workers, mostly tinsmiths. With the exception of Alfred's father, David Bower who was a joiner (just to buck the family trend). David Bower (whose parents Charles Bower and Napalina (nee Dawson) Bower came from Stockport, Cheshire) was married to Amey Teal who was born in Yorkshire.

Margaret Ellen Parr was to the daughter of a tinplater, Joseph Parr who came from Neston, Cheshire as was his own father, also called Joseph born in the early 1800's. Interestingly, the 1871 census for Joseph Parr shows him and his family living at **16 Star Street, Dingle**. Later and purely by coincidence, in 1901 the Starkey family themselves lived at 50 and then 52 Star Street Dingle a while later. Alfred and Margaret Bower are both buried in Toxteth Park Cemetery S14 No:49. Joseph Parr died in 1881 and is buried at Toxteth Park S11 No: 972.

Chapter 10 – The Starkey Family Tree

Ringo was born Richard Starkey, son of Richard Henry Starkey and yet he has always admitted that he knew his family real name is Parkin. I've always been curious about this change of surname and the many theories of why it changed. It was only when I casually re-visited a photograph I took of his paternal grandfather's gravestone a little while ago, that I found some details which didn't ring true in the recorded family history and so I realised that the Starkey family tree needed further investigation. As a result, I've done a bit of further research regarding the Starkey family and as a result I've found a wealth of information never known before which tells a very tragic, humbling and yet fascinating story of the Ringo's family past and confirms his correct surname once and for all. It's a long story that definitely needs telling so I suggest you get a cup of tea and relax in a comfy chair first before you read the next bit.

I visited Allerton Cemetery in 2015, where a lot of Beatle-related gravesites are, as I have done many times. On this occasion, I went there to photograph the resting place of Ringo's paternal grandfather John Starkey in the Church of England plot Section 31 No: 258. In 2019, I checked the photograph again and noticed the grave has four occupants. The first is John Starkey who died 3 October 1959 and reached the grand age of 73. The grave also includes his dear wife Annie (nee Bower) who died 7 February 1962, plus baby, May who was one of the four children the couple had, (including Ringo's father Richard Henry Starkey). The other occupant of the grave plot with John Starkey was Mary "mother of above", who died 11 December 1931. I didn't question this until I came across the funeral order book record held in Liverpool Record Office which showed the funeral receipt for the burial of John Starkey in 1959. The receipt quoted John's burial as "subsequent", so in other words, he was added to the plot containing his mother. I've read a lot of Beatle history from many world experts in the subject and it was more or less understood that Mary originally married a man called John Parkin, whose family hailed from Hull. John Parkin it's been reported, was a lightshipman by trade. They lived in the Dingle and from her marriage, she had a son also called John Parkin. Sometime in the early 1900's, Mary Parkin became a widow and later changed her surname to Starkey, supposedly because she was having an affair with a married man. Out of curiosity, I checked the births deaths and marriage records for the mother shown who died on 11 December 1931 and one thing led to another as they say. As far as I could tell, this Mary Parkin was not the same person. So for clarity I'll summarise what I know for both of them and you can be the judge.

Mary Elizabeth James was born in 1868, the daughter of Thaddeus James and Sarah Jane Steele. They lived at 2 Prince Edwin Lane Everton. Thaddeus came from Clonlaheen, Kilmaley, County Clare, Ireland and he was a baker by trade and Roman Catholic. In 1871, the couple moved to 2, Nest View Terrace Everton but by 1881 Mary lived with her aunty and uncle at 97B Canterbury Street Everton recorded as a "servant" on the census for that year. By 1886, the records show she was now living at 9 Corwen Terrace, Everton and it was here she met her future husband George Henry Parkin, who was living next door at 7, Corwen Terrace, Everton.

George Henry Parkin was born in Birkenhead in 1866, the son of Samuel and Mary Parkin. His father, Samuel, was a blacksmith/striker by trade and was himself born in Sheffield, Yorkshire. His wife Mary (nee Preston) was born in Middlesbrough.

Sam Parkin's own father was also a journeyman blacksmith who had originally hailed from the Isle of Wight. Sam married Mary in Liverpool in 1864, both being resident in Gregson Street Liverpool at the time but moving over the water to Birkenhead shortly after. At that time, Birkenhead was a busy industrial hub for shipbuilding and trade and so from the early 1800's, the town was rapidly developed to accommodate the expected intake of cheap labour it needed to build ships and so journeymen trades like shipwrights, blacksmiths and all converged on booming Birkenhead. As a result, thousands of terraced houses were built to accommodate them. In the north end of Birkenhead a series of tenements were erected known as the "Dock Cottages". Set close to the railway and dock systems it housed hundreds of families and the conditions were poor. The area was renowned for its poor housing, right up until the late 1960's in fact.

Nearer the Woodside ferry facing Liverpool was the area known as Lower Tranmere, where strings of poor quality housing were also built for the workers, literally yards from the industrial areas containing gasworks, smelting plants, refuse tips, graving docks, tanneries, abattoirs and glue works notwithstanding the smoke and noise pollution of the shipyards that came with it. Following the prospect of work, the Parkin family moved to 8 St Mary's Gate, Birkenhead. There was no real choice of accommodation as you had to live near to where the work was and so the family and families like them, moved continuously. They also had to take on lodgers to earn a living and by 1881 the Parkin family were now living in a tiny terraced house at 45 Thomas Street, Birkenhead with three boarders staying there too, who also all worked at the docks like George Parkin.

In 1881, Mary James father, Thaddeus James (known as John James) had re-married and they moved over to Lower Tranmere, living at 6, Barstons Buildings, Tranmere which sounds grander than it was. The neighbourhoods were tightly packed, not surprisingly overcrowded and unsanitary and subsequently, diseases such as whooping cough and bronchitis were rife. Several medical boards wrote about the environment and slum conditions of Birkenhead and the high mortality rates due to the poor living conditions there and the illnesses and disease that came from the visiting ships too. Lower Tranmere was more or less a mirror image of Dingle, both being industrials centres, both with large working class populations working at their neighbourhood docks and both with poor housing, associated health issues and high mortality rates and set apart only by the polluted River Mersey between them.

For some reason, in 1886 George Henry Parkin was living in Liverpool at 7 Corwen Terrace, Everton. It here on 8 March 1886 that he married Mary Elizabeth James at St Timothy's Church, Everton, in a Church of England wedding. George and Mary were illiterate it seems and signed their marriage certificate with an "X". On 1st August 1886 they had their first child together, John George Parkins (as spelt) who was born at 7, Rose Cottages, St Pauls Road, Lower Tranmere, Birkenhead. (**This was Ringo Starr's paternal grandfather**). John Parkin was baptised back at St Timothy's Church, Everton.

The church baptism record reports that George Henry Parkin was a "Labourer" and that their address was 59, Canterbury Street which may have been quoted for convenience or connected with Mary's own relatives. These records chop and change with the spelling of the surname on various records and census reports. It is quoted as Parkins or Parkin and even Parkinson on one occasion and being unschooled, it was impossible for Mary or George to notice. The correct surname is Parkin.

1891 was a terrible year for Mary Elizabeth Parkin. In this year the family had moved to another terraced house at 26, Princes Place, Lower Tranmere. George was now a "Driller" by trade, meaning he put holes in metalwork for rivets to be placed which were used to build ships and it was extremely dangerous, hard work. By now, they now had another two children, Mary Jane Parkin born in 1889 and Samuel Joseph Parkin born 1891. In addition, they shared their home with Mary's father, Thaddeus, her own brother Michael (another driller), George's aunty Agnes and a boarder (another driller). Their house was set close to the graving docks and the polluted river, like many folk in the bustling slum neighbourhood and so when disease struck, it could affect the entire street. On 1st October 1891 Mary Parkins' father Thaddeus died aged 63, causes unknown, but most likely bronchitis, because less than a week later on 7th October George Henry Parkin died of pleurisy and pneumonia at home. He was only 26 years old. Mary his wife, was present at the death.

The sudden death of Mary's father and then her own husband in October 1891 must have been traumatic. She was 23 years old, bringing up 3 young children and had lodger relatives with no money coming in. Early deaths, infant mortality and associated life-long illnesses were not uncommon in industrial places like this. There was no healthcare or welfare system to help and so her father Thaddeus James was buried on 9 October 1891 in a pauper's grave at Bebington Cemetery, Town Lane, Bebington Section F Grave No: 308 in the Roman Catholic section. The next day 10 October 1891 George Henry Parkin was buried at Bebington Cemetery in another pauper's grave at Section F Grave No: 314 in the Church of England section. Both graves were shared with two other persons, not related or connected to them, though they appear to be from the same street or nearby in Tranmere, so this may have been a disease outbreak of some kind. There are no gravestones or remnant markers for either one.

In early 1892 and now living at 4, Quigley Street Tranmere, Mary had a further tragic loss when her youngest son Samuel Joseph Parkin died only 13 months old on 30 April 1892. He too was buried in Bebington Cemetery C of E section Section F Plot 314, in a pauper's grave with four other children. This left Mary with her two remaining children, John George Parkin aged 5 and Mary Jane Parkin aged 2. It was a hard life for all working class people in Birkenhead and all industrial cities in Great Britain at that time, and life was short and expendable, as it proved to be for Mary Parkin's family.

In late 1892 however, Mary and her family were resident at a new address, 3, Halkyn Place, Birkenhead. (Probably Halkin Place). On 10 October 1892 (the first anniversary of her late husband's funeral), she re-married. She married Richard Henry Starkey, a 26 year old bachelor, who was also by profession, a driller, like her late husband. They married at nearby St John's Church, Huskisson Street, Birkenhead.

Richard Henry Starkey was born in 1866 in Birkenhead. His father was also called Richard Henry Starkey and was a journeyman carpenter by trade, born in Lezayre, Ramsay, Isle of Man. In 1866, the Starkey family resided at 16, Queens' Buildings (Rhodeus Place) Birkenhead situated in the "North End" of Birkenhead at the "Dock Cottages" tenements, where lots of other journeymen and their families lived. Like many other working class families, they moved a lot. By 1871 the family re-located to 21 Taylors Buildings, Oliver Lane, Birkenhead, nearer to the docks and the next census reported yet another move down to the dockside slums of 7, Elizabeth Place, Birkenhead, yards from a huge gasometer, a series of train engine sheds, numerous ironworks and docks. Pictures exist of the actual address on the internet of the street. The 1891 census then reveals an interesting fact about Richard Starkey before he married. In 1882, he enlisted as a soldier and joined the infantry. (More on this later.)

In October 1892, Richard Henry Starkey and Mary Elizabeth Parkin (nee James) married. Mary is declared as a widow on the marriage certificate. Significantly, she brought with her John George Parkin and Mary Jane Parkin from her previous marriage and so these became Richard H Starkey's step children.

Perhaps the living conditions or work prospects were making it hard for the Starkey family in Birkenhead because by 1894 the family had moved away to rural North Wales as they re-located to a small hamlet at Tan Y Clawdd Cottages, Johnstown, near Ruabon, Denbighshire. Johnstown has a coal mine and is near to the famous Ruabon Quarries. Richard worked there as a Fitters' labourer. It was also there were they had their first child together Ann Jane Maud Starkey. The work didn't last so long as they'd wished as the whole family returned to Tranmere in 1896 and moved into 40 Rosslyn Street, Lower Tranmere, Birkenhead. Once back, there followed the births of more children, namely Sarah Agnes Starkey in 1895 and Beatrice May Starkey in 1898.

Nothing is known about the family whereabouts in 1899 but the subsequent records found from 1900 onwards show that the family moved home many times and importantly moved over the water to live in the Dingle in the district of Toxteth, Liverpool.

The first record of 1900 found is a baptism record for another child born. In October 1900 Eleanor Pretoria Starkey was baptised at St James Church, Toxteth Park. The Starkey family were then living at 205, Grafton Street, Liverpool. Her middle name of Pretoria shows the clear influence of the Boer War which was occurring at the time, (much like John Winston Lennon being named as World War 2 began). Her father had actually taken part in the Boer War, so this was the other reason she was so named.

The 1901 census reports a very interesting new address for the family and even more interesting details. In 1901, the Starkey's were now living at 52, Star Street, Dingle. Mary quoted her name as "Polly". The name of Polly is a pet variant of Mary (Molly). John George Parkin was still living with his mother, but now working as a Steel Rivet Handler. Mary (Parkin) Starkey's brother, Michael was still living with them all and was still a Driller by trade. Mary's husband Richard Henry Starkey is not declared on the census this time. That's because he was back to being a soldier and away from home. He did return shortly after the census report and that's evident from the birth of their next (5th) child Richard Henry Buller Starkey baptised October 1902. The middle name of Buller is another patriotic Boer War reference of Sir Redvers Buller, a General in the British Army who served as Commander in Chief of the British Forces in South Africa during the early part of the second Boer War. At the time of Richard Junior's baptism at St Gabriel's Church, Toxteth, the family had moved again to the empty property of 50 Star Street, Dingle. The baptism record also reveals Richard Henry Starkey was now reported as a "Soldier".

William John Starkey was the next addition to the Starkey clan born in February 1904. By this time Richard had returned from the army and was a "driller" once again. Ever mobile, the Starkey family moved a few doors down to now live at 46, Star Street, Dingle by this time. In August 1907 another child Sadie Starkey was born but oddly, she was baptised in a Wesleyan Methodist Hall in Lancaster, quite some distance from Liverpool for reasons unknown.

There's still a bit of the Starkey Story to go but it's now worth detailing the interesting history of Richard Henry Starkey – soldier. For this information I'm extremely indebted to Nick Metcalfe, a renowned war historian and Boer War specialist who found a lot of the details for me.

Richard Henry Starkey had a long and complicated military background which covered a long period of time, almost 35 years. He originally enlisted into the 3rd (Militia) Battalion of The North Staffordshire Regiment on 22 September 1882 before enlisting into the Regular Army (same regiment) on 22 September 1884 aged 18 (his birthday) His number was 1323. He deserted on 4 October 1884.

He then 'fraudulently enlisted' into The Royal Inniskilling Fusiliers using the name 'John Roberts' on 10 October 1884 and was numbered 1185. Within a few days, he was found out and held in custody pending court martial. He was released rather than tried and served in his own name having forfeited all previous service towards his engagement. He was discharged 'time expired' (i.e. at the end of his 12 year's engagement) in 1896.

Richard was then mobilised from the reserve in December 1899 for service in South Africa. He served there with the 1st Battalion from his arrival with one of the reinforcement drafts in March 1900 to September 1901; luckily missing the earlier battles in which the Battalion suffered severely. He is on the Inniskilling's medal roll for South Africa in his own name. He was awarded the Queen's South Africa Medal with clasps 'Belfast' 'Natal' & 'South Africa 1901'. On his return he was discharged in October 1901.

He next enlisted into the Royal Garrison Regiment in July 1902, numbered 5392, and was posted to the 5th Battalion. It's presumed he joined it in Nova Scotia, Canada. He was discharged 'time expired' in 1904. He then re-enlisted into the Royal Inniskilling Fusiliers Militia (from 1908 known as the Special Reserve) at Birkenhead on 23 March 1905. He was discharged at the end of his engagement on 22 March 1909.

He even enlisted during the First World War in February 1915 and joined the Royal Engineers (numbered 78769) and served in UK at the 2nd Reserve Battalion at Chattenden but fell sick and was discharged in May 1917. He was awarded the Silver War Badge number 170184 and given an army pension, which he collected all his remaining life from Park Place, Dingle Post Office.

So in short, Richard Henry Starkey was a regular solder (recalled reservist) in the Boer War with 1st Inniskilling in 1900 and 1901 and then joined the Royal Garrison Regiment in 1902 after he returned. He served in the UK in the First World War and was pensioned off.

Between the 2nd Boer War and First World War Richard Henry Starkey returned to his trade as a Driller and bringing up his family. They had an eighth child together (Marys' 11th) called Thaddeus James Starkey (after Mary's late father) in 1910 but he sadly died as a baby and was buried at Toxteth Cemetery, Section 10 Grave 131 Church of England consecrated section.

The Starkey family had numerous house moves during this period as the Voters Lists for the district show, living at 77 Upper Essex Street Dingle, then 25 Mornington Street, Dingle, then 17, Vere Street, Dingle, where the family finally settled. By 1909, Mary's first son, John George Parkin had finally left the family home.

On 31 July 1910 John Parkin Starkey (23) as he was now stated on the marriage banns for St Matthews Church married Annie Bower (22). John's father is reported on the banns as "Henry Parkin Starkey" occupation "Driller". John's then address was quoted as 31, Robinson Street Dingle. Richard Henry Starkey was John's step-father and so this name is incorrect. In addition, there is no such street or variations on any historic records for "Robinson Street, Dingle". It's not certain why this was done. This mild deception was not important but in 1914 and 1918, the Vicar of St Matthews, Theodore A Howard married Richard H Starkey's' oldest daughters, Ann and Sarah and in such a close neighbourhood, should have known something was afoot.

The 1911 census is most revealing of all for John Starkey. He reports his home address as 21 Vere Street and he lived there with Annie Starkey (Nee Bower) and her sister/boarder. On this record, John here quotes his name as "John George Starkey" and appears to have dropped the Parkin surname. He also quotes his birthplace as Birkenhead, Cheshire. They later moved to 59, Madryn Street, Dingle.

John and Annie Starkey then brought up four of their own children John A Starkey, May Starkey (who died as a child), Nancy Starkey, (known as "Ann") and Richard Henry Starkey who later married Elsie Gleaves and in 1940 he became the father of Richard Starkey also known as Ringo Starr.

On 31 July 1926 Mary Elizabeth Starkey's second husband Richard Henry Starkey died of prolonged chronic bronchitis and heart failure. He was 59 years old. Mary was present at his death at 17, Vere Street, Dingle. He was buried on 5 August 1926 at 3pm at Allerton Cemetery, Section 22 Grave No: 269 in the Church of England consecrated section.

His step-son John Parkin Starkey (Ringo's granddad) paid for the burial. The Undertakers were William McLean & Sons Ltd, 206, Windsor Street, Dingle, Liverpool 8. The cost of burial was £1. The minister for the burial was John E Houghton, Vicar from St Gabriel's Church, Dingle. His clerical fees were 7 shillings and sixpence. The grave appears to be a subsequent one according to records, but no other details of who is buried there too are known. I've visited the cemetery, but never found a gravestone or similar for him. There is a new gravestone for another person there now. Allerton Cemetery has confirmed that the plot is correct however.

Mary Elizabeth Starkey lived until 13 December 1931, aged 64 years. She suffered many losses and tragedies in her life and yet survived against the odds. All her surviving children married and raised their own families, including one very famous individual great grandson who by the coincidences and circumstances of Mary's extra ordinary life has enjoyed his own extra ordinary life. The story of Mary James reveals many new facts about the Starkey family such as the Irish connection which was only previously thought to be quite a distant relative who came from County Mayo. In addition, the issue of mixed faith marriages which later bothered Ringo and Geraldine McGovern, his first fiancée, certainly seems to have been prevalent in the time of Mary and George Henry Parkin and even her second husband Richard. Added to the sad fact that pleurisy and pneumonia which killed George Henry Parkin, also affected a young Richard "Ringo" Starkey but he thankfully survived it. Ringo even went to the Isle of Man as a teenager with his grandparents which may have a slight connection with John Starkey's own step-fathers' history. The colourful life of Richard Henry Starkey travelling the world as a soldier is possibly one of the most unexpected surprises I've found all whilst basically trying to unravel the mystery of John Starkey's gravestone.

The other Mary Parkin

To be fair, I have also fully investigated the details of the other person called Mary Parkin but try as I might I couldn't get the details to fit, though some coincidences appeared, that's all they simply were. Here's what I found.

Mary Ann Ley was born 21 January 1868 and lived at 40 Beresford Road, Toxteth. She married John Parkin born in 1865 and he lived at 19, Flint Street, Liverpool by Queens Dock. John Parkin's family came from Hull and were seafarers. John Parkin was a lightshipman by trade. In 1890, they had a son John Parkin (Junior) and in 1892 a daughter Ethel Parkin was born. By this time, they were living at 55 Merlin Street, Toxteth and a short while later, they moved out of Dingle to live at 195 Netherfield Road, Everton. During this period John Parkin Senior doesn't appear on the census records. Whereabouts are unknown. By 1901, the Parkin family were a family unit once again, this time now living back in Dingle at 42, Madryn Street, the street were Ringo Starr was born. In 1903, John Parkin (Senior) unfortunately died. References in many Beatle books suggest this was a period from 1903 until approximately 1911 when 33 year old Mary (Ley) Parkin may have had an illicit affair with a married man surname of Starkey and for the convenience and sake of a scandal, she took his surname which her son took on also. The 1911 census reports that her son John Parkin was an apprentice engineer by trade. It is known that Ringo's paternal grandfather was a boilermaker not an engineer. The record also shows at this time that the family returned to Mary (Ley) Parkin's childhood home at 40 Beresford Road, Everton. From 1920 onwards Mary (Ley) Parkin lived above a grocers shop at 29, Dingle Lane, Dingle, owned by her daughter Ethel and her husband Henry LYTH. At the start of wartime in 1939 Mary was 71 years old and she moved over the water to the safer backwater of 87, Pensby Road, Heswall, Wirral, well away from the blitzed docklands of Birkenhead and Liverpool. This time she was living above another shop run by Mr & Mrs Lyth and living by "private means" according to the 1939 Register available. Mary died at the grand age of 82 in 1950 and was buried at Toxteth Cemetery Section 5 No: 284 Church of England.

If Mary Ley Parkin had "private means" to live she was well-off and I think this discounts her and her son from the Starkey story who clearly had a very hard, poor upbringing. The brief move to Madryn Street may have seemed an encouraging clue but her son's trade goes against the grain of proof for the Mary James Parkin Starkey version. To top it off, John Parkin Starkey's' gravestone gives the final big clue as Mary (Ley) Parkin didn't die in 1931 but Mary (James) STARKEY did.

Aunty Edey & Harry Graves

Going into so much depth over the Starkey story I couldn't help tackling some other Starkey history along the way. One story concerns Ringo's own step-father, Harry Graves, who almost never married Ringo's mother Elsie.

Ringo's father was Richard Henry Starkey and he had two sisters, May (died young) and Nancy (known as "Ann") and a brother, John Alfred. John married Edith Jones in 1934. Edith lived at 13, Ruby Street, Dingle and when they married they moved to 42, Parkhill Road, Dingle. In 1943, John died, cause unknown. In 1945, probably right after the war, Harry Graves arrived from Romford, East London, looking for work on Merseyside. Harry was a very likeable chap and blended in very easily amongst the Dingle neighbourhood. He firstly lodged at 86 Admiral Street, Dingle and it wasn't long before he took an interest in the widower Edith "Edey" Starkey and they began to see each other. In doing so, they may have met with Elsie Starkey (nee Gleave) who had been separated from Richard H Starkey since 1943. Elsie it seems, was dating a local widower called Joe Taylor who lived at 14, Erith Street, Dingle. Joe was a tram conductor according to records held. However, Harry had clearly taken a liking to Elsie, though he was taking Edey out and sometime in early 1946 things changed. Seemingly by mutual agreement, Harry stopped seeing Edey and Elsie stopped seeing Joe and they simply swapped dating partners. In August 1946, Edey Starkey married Joe Taylor at a registry office and lived at 32, Ruby Street right up until the 1970's. Harry meanwhile carried on dating Elsie and up until 1950 he lived at 2, Jacob Street, Liverpool 8. In 1953 they finally married, much to everyone's approval. Aunty Edey and Uncle Joe were two of Ringo's favourite relatives and he visited them often.

As a footnote, my research on the Starkey story has shown that although Ringo's father left the family at 9 Madryn Street in 1943 and apparently "moved away", the Voters Register for the area shows that he was registered at his parents' home at the bottom of the same street at 59, Madryn Street. Odder still, Ringo still appeared on local voters list registers as living at 10, Admiral Grove, Dingle right up until 1965.

Chapter 11 - Bonus Track - Brian Epstein's Family Tree

I've already said that each of the Beatles' family trees unfolds a story with so many twists and turns, tragedies and surprises that without a single one of them so much could have been so different. Let's not therefore neglect the role of Brian Epstein who also made The Beatles as big as they became. The Epstein story, like John, Paul, George and Ringo, depended on immigrants coming to the United Kingdom. In this case with the Epstein family tree it was to avoid Russian pogroms and persecution in their home countries, added to which they didn't even speak English and so I looked into the back story of Brian Epstein's ancestors. It's a far briefer rendition than the band's family trees as records don't exist for many of his East European ancestors, but worth a mention nonetheless.

Brian Samuel Epstein was born September 1934 in Liverpool. His parents were Harry (1904-1967) and Malka Epstein (1914-1996) who married in 1933. They also had another son, Clive John Epstein born in 1934. (died 1988)

Harry Epstein was born in Liverpool in 1904 the son of émigré Isaac Epstein (1879-1955). Harry ran the family furniture dealers started by his father, called Epstein's. The family originally lived at 80 Walton Road, above their shop and then moved to 24 Rockfield Road, Anfield. The family consisted of father Isaac, wife Dinah (1880-1955) and children, Sarah, Leslie (Lazarus), Harry, Gertrude. They also had a housekeeper/domestic from Dingle called Sarah Swain (1889) living in. (she later emigrated herself to Quebec April 1912 on S.S Lake Manitoba from Liverpool.)

After sons Harry and Leslie joined the family firm, Isaac Epstein founded "I. Epstein and Sons", and enlarged his furniture business by taking over adjacent shops (62/72 Walton Road) to sell a varied range of other goods, such as musical instruments and household appliances. They called the expanding business NEMS (North End Music Stores) which offered lenient credit terms, and from which McCartney's father Jim, once bought a piano.

Malka "Queenie/Minnie" Epstein was born Malka Hyman in Sheffield. Her parents were Louis Hyman (1879-1952) and Annie Rachel Hyman (nee Kimise) (1883-1944) who were both émigrés from Russia. Louis came from Sopatecin, Suwalki, Russia. Annie's parents Yaakov and Frieda Koomis remained in Russia. Louis was a cabinet maker and by 1905 was running a cabinet making factory. They were made British subjects in 1911. They even had a telephone in 1911, living at 67 Montgomery Terrace, Sheffield. The family consisted of Barnet, Frieda (2) and Minnie/Malka. By 1919 Louis Hyman was running The Sheffield Cabinet Manufacturing Company. He died in 1952.

Harry Epstein's father Isaac Epstein came from Zavoda, Konstantinovo, Russia, and located 100km south east of Moscow. He left Russia to escape the pogroms and came to Liverpool. He married Dinah Hyman in 1900 in Prestwich. Dinah was born in Cheetham, Manchester. Her parents were Joseph Hyman (1849- 1920) and Esther Hyman (1852-1932) from Plonsk, Mazowiekie, Poland and were naturalised in the United Kingdom in 1894 settling in Manchester. Joseph was the son of Harris and Sarah Hyman. Joseph was a draper. The family consisted of children, Hannah, Dinah, Rachel, Leah, Saul, Sarah.

At the outbreak of WW2, Queenie and her young sons, Brian and Clive were evacuated and relocated to Prestatyn, North Wales (as was Beatle assistant Neil Aspinall). During World War 2, the Epstein's then moved to Southport where Brian went to two schools and expelled him for laziness and poor performance. The Epstein family returned to Liverpool in 1945 and settled in South Liverpool at 197 Queens Drive, Childwall, Liverpool, living there for 30 years. Brian was sent to numerous boarding schools after that but he didn't aspire in any of them. He wanted to be dress designer but father Harry refused and after National Service and a failed attempt at an acting profession, Brian settled to be Harry's successor with his brother managing NEMS in Liverpool city centre. Then, in November 1961 he saw the Beatles playing one wet afternoon in the Cavern and that changed everything. The rest you probably know.

Acknowledgements & Thanks

Liverpool Central Library Archive Team- Always helpful and patient- very appreciated.

Wirral Archives Team—Very supportive with all kinds of emails and enquiries from yours truly.

Mark Glinister- Beatles fan, ELO nut and podcaster who came on a few exploratory days out to places far and wide and near and even just around the corner. Ta la.

Mark Lewisohn- THE best Beatles author and researcher bar none. Cheers for the kind comments, help, encouragement and support (I'll always wear it).

Dr.Steven D Knott- (1960-2021) a great human being, musician, geologist, good laugh and friend.

Printed in Great Britain
by Amazon